People of a
Compassionate God

PEOPLE OF A COMPASSIONATE GOD

Creating Welcoming Congregations

EDITED BY
JANET FORSYTHE FISHBURN

Abingdon Press
Nashville

PEOPLE OF A COMPASSIONATE GOD:
CREATING WELCOMING CONGREGATIONS

Copyright © 2003 by Abingdon Press

This book is printed on acid-free paper.

Library of Congress Cataloging-in-Publication Data

People of a compassionate God: creating welcoming congregations / Janet Forsythe Fishburn, editor.
    p. cm.
Includes bibliographical references (p.   ).
ISBN 0-687-02324-6 (Binding: Adhesive : alk. paper)
1.Homosexuality—Religious aspects—United Methodist Church (U.S.)
2. United Methodist Church (U.S.)—Membership. I. Fishburn, Janet Forsythe, 1937-

BX8385.H6P46 2003
253—dc21
                                                    2003009635

The song on pages 105 and 106 is "Part of the Family," words and music © Copyright 1984 by James K. Manley [www.manleymusic. com].

Scripture quotations are from the *New Revised Standard Version of the Bible,* copyright © 1989, by the Division of Christian Education of the National Council of the Churches of Christ in the United States of America. Used by permission. All rights reserved.

The song on page 107 is "Shalom to You," words © 1983 The United Methodist Publishing House.

03 04 05 06 07 08 09 10 11 12—10 9 8 7 6 5 4 3 2 1
MANUFACTURED IN THE UNITED STATES OF AMERICA

CONTENTS

110268

PROLOGUE

People of a Compassionate God: Creating Welcoming Congregations had its origins in two Consultations sponsored by The United Methodist Association of Scholars of Christian Education (UMASCE) held in August 1996 and August 1997. We began the congregational research described here during the two three-day meetings. In 1996 we were prepared by two consultants "to gather and interpret information about what happens when a congregation and its members undertake to learn and teach about an identified issue." In the year between the meetings, we began our research with five congregations that had explored membership in the Reconciling Congregation Program. Our first drafts were discussed at the 1997 meeting. Our "identified issue" was homosexuality. Other teams of researchers prepared reports on family ministries and decision making through spiritual discernment.

Our approach to congregational research was informed and shaped by theologian Bernard Cooke and anthropologist Peter Stromberg. Both have contributed to studies in their respective fields that include significant attention to the symbolism of words, events, places, and people. In the first Consultation, Peter coached us on a participant-observer approach to learning about the story and environment of a congregation. Bernard cultivated our sensitivity to the variety of ways that people express beliefs and theology in congregational settings. In the second Consultation, they were patient and wise critics of our initial descriptions of these congregations.

The two Consultations and a later meeting of our group to identify themes in our research were supported by a generous grant administered by Dorothy Bass through The Valparaiso Project of the Lilly Foundation. We are grateful for her careful reading of our research proposal and subsequent interactions with us as we worked on this book. She contributed provocative questions about what we were learning as our work continued. A second team meeting, in which we discussed how to interpret what we had learned and then outlined book chapters, was funded by the Louisville Institute and administered by congregational researcher James W. Lewis. We are grateful to him for his encouragement and perceptive comments about our research and writing in its final phases.

Chapters 2 through 6 are descriptions of five United Methodist congregations which we believe will be a valuable guide for clergy and lay leaders of any congregation coping with demands for change. Chapters 7 through 9 reflect our group discussions and conclusions about how these congregations engaged difficult issues through study and dialogue and how they made difficult decisions. These conclusions are supported by in-depth studies of several other Reconciling Congregations and information gathered through a questionnaire from an additional thirty-one congregations that participated in the Reconciling Congregation Program (see appendix 1).

Our descriptions of the congregations come from church documents and interviews we conducted. Many of the quotations in the book reflect the enthusiasm and commitment of pastors and members of the congregations and some of the quotations contain colloquial language.

We want to thank all of the pastors and lay leaders of the five congregations for their willingness to be interviewed, their assistance in helping us formulate the story of their congregation, and their permission to tell their story in print. We also want to thank several graduate students who assisted us in our research and discussions about what we had learned.

I have coordinated the work of our team from the beginning. In that capacity, and as the editor of our book, I have been dazzled and blessed by the variety of gifts, knowledge, and insights brought to our work by each woman. I am grateful to Mary Elizabeth Moore, Elizabeth Box Price, Nelle Slater, and Linda Vogel for their research, writing, good advice, and sustaining interest in our project over an eight year period.

Janet Forsythe Fishburn

ABOUT THE AUTHORS

Janet Forsythe Fishburn is Professor Emerita of Teaching Ministries at The Theological School of Drew University in Madison, New Jersey. She is an ordained member of Newton Presbytery, Presbyterian Church, U.S.A.

Debora Agra Junker participated in discussions about the research on two occasions when she was a doctoral candidate at Garrett-Evangelical Theological Seminary in Evanston, Illinois. She was awarded her Ph.D. in 2003 and now teaches in her home city of Sao Paulo (San Palo), Brazil.

Steve Marlatt teaches history at Fontana High School in California, having taught junior and senior high school social sciences for 25 years. He is active in Claremont United Methodist Church's Reconciling Ministries and in Parents, Families and Friends of Lesbians and Gays (PFLAG).

Gabriele Mayer contributed to the study of the Claremont United Methodist Church while a doctoral candidate at the Claremont School of Theology in California. She completed her Ph.D. in 2003 and returned to her native Germany where she teaches, serves as diaconal minister, and is Secretary of the Women's and Gender Desk at EMS, an ecumenical association.

Mary Elizabeth Moore is Professor of Religion and Education at Candler School of Theology, where she is also Director of Women in Theology and Ministry. She is an ordained deacon of the California-Pacific Annual Conference of The United Methodist Church.

Elizabeth Box Price is Professor of Christian Religious Education at Phillips Theological Seminary in Tulsa, Oklahoma. She is an ordained deacon of the Oklahoma Conference of The United Methodist Church.

Nelle G. Slater is Professor Emerita of Christian Education and Lois and Dale Bright Professor of Christian Ministries at Christian Theological Seminary in Indianapolis, Indiana.

Linda Vogel is Professor of Christian Education at Garrett-Evangelical Theological Seminary in Evanston, Illinois. She is an ordained deacon of the Iowa Annual Conference of The United Methodist Church.

CHAPTER ONE

INTRODUCTION: A GUIDE TO CONGREGATIONAL CHANGE

The Methodist Church split in 1844—largely over slavery. The Civil Rights movement of the 1950s and 1960s again caused stress and conflict in many faith communities. Perhaps no other issue since that time has put as much stress on congregations (and all social institutions including families, the military, education, the business world, health care, and so forth) until the 1990s, when attitudes and policies dealing with homosexuality began to be challenged by persons of faith.

How do congregations cope with demands for deep change? What are some of the strategies that foster open dialogue and make room at the table for diverse voices and lifestyles? What behaviors and strategies build walls and alienate those who call for change? It was questions like these that five Christian educators decided to examine. Perhaps, we thought, we can learn about helping congregations deal with conflict and change by studying congregations that have wrestled with this highly emotional issue.

Our overarching question was to learn all we could about how faith communities engage issues that go to the very heart of faith and beliefs. How do people learn to speak the truth (as they see it) in love and to listen to others whose commitments and sense of the gospel are diametrically opposed to their beliefs? How can the Bible be a resource for honest exploration? When does the Bible become a weapon to use against those who differ in their understanding of gospel demands? What is the role of science and medicine and the social sciences in seeking to understand human sexuality? What role ought individual experiences and stories play in helping us to see more clearly? How do individuals and communities discern God's will in ways that build up and do not tear down the faith community?

We each chose a congregation where we would have access to lay and clergy leadership and where we could engage in participant observation. Some of us studied our own congregation; others did not. Our goal was to identify five very different faith communities in different locales and to seek permission to study them and their processes as they considered the feasibility of change in attitudes and policies that block homosexual persons from ordination and label their sexual orientation as "incompatible with Christian teaching."

We chose congregations that we knew had at least a small group that was committed to inviting or challenging the congregation into a study of homosexuality and to consider becoming a Reconciling Congregation—a congregation that welcomes all persons as equals, including those who are gay, lesbian, bisexual, or transgendered. Our goal was to study the processes they used and to invite pastors and laity to reflect on these processes. What opened doors? What closed doors? What strategies invited honest dialogue and allowed for the expression of differing opinions?

What strategies proved to foster conflict and bad feelings? How was a decision for the congregation to become or not become a Reconciling Congregation made? Who participated in the decision-making process?

How do congregations deal faithfully with honest differences? During the formative years of the Christian church, certainly Peter and Paul had to wrestle with core differences. The question is not new. The church at the time of the Reformation struggled with different priorities and commitments. How does one look at theological differences and at the same time recognize the role power and control play in such divisive issues?

With these questions in mind, we selected a well-established suburban congregation in New York state, a high-steeple congregation in the heart of a medium-sized midwestern city, a small, struggling interracial congregation in a large and once-affluent building in the Edgewater neighborhood in Chicago, a missional community established by the Oklahoma Annual Conference in Tulsa to address needs of gay, lesbian, bisexual, and transgendered persons in that city, and First Church in a highly educated community in Southern California.

We soon learned that each of these congregations had identity-forming stories to tell and some person or persons(s), groups or events that introduced cognitive dissonance into the life of these faith communities. Strategies varied; questions and conflict arose. Pain was a reality for everyone actively involved in trying to discern whether or not these congregations would become affiliated with the Reconciling Congregation Program.[1]

The outcomes of the processes we studied were varied. Three congregations did vote to become Reconciling Congregations. One congregation stopped the process before a final decision could be made. The missional community reluctantly decided to disaffiliate with The United Methodist Church after the 2000 General Conference in order not to put their pastor's ordination credentials at risk.[2] They are now affiliated with the United Church of Christ.

We believe this book can serve as a guide for congregations facing deep change, that is, change that challenges deeply held convictions and requires examining many long-held assumptions. We chose the issue of homosexuality because we believe it calls into question many deeply held convictions and challenges our nation and our faith communities to consider radical new ways of seeing and believing.

We do believe that the gospel calls us as followers of Jesus Christ to be more open to difference and more inclusive in our faith walks. We care deeply for the individuals and families who are being hurt by church policies that exclude them from full participation. But this book is not about what particular individuals believe on this issue. Rather, it is about how congregations where people holding many different positions on this issue can dare to openly explore what God calls them to do and be in this time and place. How can faith communities handle conflict in respectful ways that name and face issues that are powerful enough to divide and destroy the community or, at the very least, to fracture the community?

With this goal in mind, we listened carefully to people whose views differed from each other and from ours. We discovered destructive behaviors on the part of some who favored more inclusivity and on the part of some who truly believed that The United Methodist *Discipline* is right and that the Bible sees homosexuality as sin. We found gospel values being lived by persons with different beliefs and on both sides of the issue of homosexuality and about the Reconciling Congregation Program.

It is our hope that this book will invite you into the stories, lives, questions, and struggles of congregations and individuals who were seeking to discern God's will. We hope it will challenge you to risk naming the issues that divide and block your congregation's witness in a hurting and hurtful world. Dare to walk into your questions. Dare to listen to understand rather than only to refute. Share your own stories and hopes and fears rather than speaking for others. Engage in serious Bible study. Seek out the best scientific, social scientific, and theological information that is available to inform you to make the best decisions possible for you. Listen to those who disagree and ask yourself what additional perspectives God is calling you to consider.

Many issues face faith communities as we seek to live faithfully into the twenty-first century. Since 9/11/2001, Christians are being called to face what it means to be part of a world court and community. Is it ever justifiable to use nuclear weapons? Are governments (especially ours) ever justified in assassinating those we judge to be our enemies? Are the United States and our allies justified in bombing nations that harbor terrorists? Where and in what circumstances does the gospel compel us to be countercultural and to turn the world upside-down? What might it mean to be countercultural? What does the gospel call us to do and be in a world where violence and terrorism have been loosed?

You are invited to read the five congregational stories (chapters 2–6). Listen to the joys and pains that are being expressed. Think about what actions fostered seeking to discern God's will and what actions tore down and blocked discernment that honors diverse opinions. Think about situations in your own faith community that parallel some of these experiences.

Once you have encountered these very different congregations and have their stories in mind, you are invited to reflect on what we learned as we examined the experiences of these United Methodist communities (chapters 7–9). We believe that most faith communities (especially Presbyterian, Lutheran, Baptist, Episcopal, and United Church of Christ) have congregations and issues very much like these United Methodist congregations.

What does it mean to "have ears to hear" and "eyes to see"? Where is Jesus calling our faith communities to go in these days? How can we learn from the triumphs and tragedies of these five congregations who opened themselves to scrutiny so that we might all learn how to risk walking into hard questions and the possibility of change? We hope you are blessed by this journey toward *compassion and commitment* as faithful members of congregations and denominations that seek to embody Christ's call to love our neighbor with "all our heart, mind and soul."

CHAPTER TWO

RESPONDING TO TRAGEDY AND INJUSTICE

A PROGRESSIVE, MISSION ORIENTED, LEADERSHIP CONGREGATION

It would be hard to miss the mission orientation of the Saratoga Springs United Methodist Church. Members are eager to tell visitors about the cross outside the window. Harold Smith, a retired pastor who chaired the Reconciling Congregation Task Force, remembers that "the very first Sunday we were here, one of the members saw that we were guests and put us up front so we could see the footprints in the floor going outside to the cross. That's the message in this church. We don't keep our faith in these walls. We take it outwards."[1]

This focal symbol of the congregation is also on the front of the bulletin in a drawing of the cross outside the large clear glass window. Under the cross on the bulletin are the words, "Worshiping God, Nurturing Community, Growing in Understanding, Serving the World." This brief representation of the congregation comes from a study retreat led by former pastor Bob Long in the mid-1980s about the purpose of the congregation and its use of space.

The theological commitments of the congregation are expressed on the bulletin every Sunday in words from the church mission statement formulated in 1995 when the congregation agreed to become part of the Reconciling Congregation Program:

> All persons are recipients of God's love and grace; God intends the church to be a community which embodies love, grace, and justice for all people as a sign of God's covenant. We, therefore, seek and welcome persons of any age, gender, race, ethnic background, sexual orientation, economic condition, physical or mental ability as full participants in our community of faith.

Rod Scoville, the pastor from 1963 to 1970 and now pastor emeritus, is credited by longtime members for leading the congregation into a broad commitment to world mission. Under his leadership in the mid-1960s, the congregation first identified with the cross outside the window.

It was also during the 1960s that the congregation began to consider moving its location in the business center of Saratoga Springs, a nineteenth-century summer resort town, to one of the newer residential areas on the outskirts of the city. Scoville helped the congregation understand the need to be freed of a building that was draining resources and inhibiting mission, both local and global. Until the move in the mid-1970s the congregation was the permanent meeting place of the Troy Annual Conference.[2]

Robert Trost, pastor from 1970 to 1982, led the long process preceding the move. The decision to leave the longtime historic location of the congregation was a time of controversy, pain, and anger. According to one estimate, the congregation may have lost as many as 200 of 800 members at that time. Some of that group were people who were inactive. But there were others for whom leaving the old building was a very emotional loss.

The new sanctuary, dedicated in 1976, reflects the highly democratic, inclusive nature of the congregation. The choir and pulpit are only very slightly elevated. The pastors lead part of the service from the floor in front of the pulpit. The openness of the congregation is reflected in the light, airy feel of floor to ceiling windows on two sides of the sanctuary. At the same time, the world is never far away.

Saratoga Springs United Methodist Church is now a bustling suburban congregation of almost nine hundred members from many walks of life, including professional people, educators, managers, business people, contractors, plumbers, electricians, people in construction. This mix reflects the growth of new residential areas around the older down-town core of the city. Due to the proximity of a retirement facility developed by the Troy Annual Conference, an unusual number of retired pastors and their spouses participate in the congregation, including at least two former pastors, Rod Scoville and Jane Borden (1982–1994). Since becoming a Reconciling Congregation in 1995, the congregation has become slightly more ethnically diverse and gains about 40 to 45 members a year.[3]

The present senior pastor, Bill Lasher (1994–), describes congregational commitment to missions—both global and local—as "a core value of the congregation." More than 20 percent of all the congregation's income is allocated for local and global missions. This includes a decision to tithe for local missions all income given to the building fund. Special outreach projects often capture the imagination and tap the generosity of the congregation. For example, in a recent year the Sunday school and adults raised more than $25,000 to purchase animals for people in poor countries through Heifer International.

Lasher points out that Saratoga Springs is also a "leadership church," a congregation with many members who provide leadership in their conference, their congregation, and their community. Members are leaders in Troy Conference, in United Methodist Women, in local missions like domestic violence services, soup kitchens, a homeless center and local politics, in addition to the congregation's long-term commitment to global missions. These are people generous with both time and resources.

Lasher describes his role in this "leadership congregation" as that of a facilitator and resource person. When several mothers of preschool children requested a church program to meet their needs, he helped them launch a group called Lambs. The group for preschool children and their mothers now meets at the church four mornings a week. The founders of Lambs were amazed to learn that a new program could be started without first being scrutinized by some church committee.

The congregation is known in Saratoga Springs for its youth programs, its mission outreach, and since 1995, for its inclusivity. Harold Smith says that:

> People feel free to offer leadership in every field from technology and computers to the most humble people needing help. That kind of leadership has predisposed this congregation to be doing as an active, progressive, liberal community. And it's not where the Methodist Church has been for the last sixty years. This church is a definite anomaly.

Morale among members is high. They are proud of their reputation as a mission congregation. A. C. Riley, a member of the Reconciling Congregation Task Force, describes the mission of the congregation in terms of inclusiveness, peace, and justice, and "opening our doors to people who are needy." This long history of justice-seeking, of attention to social issues, of progressive outlook, helps explain why participation in the Reconciling Congregation Program is regarded as one of the congregation's missions and as "just another justice issue."

There is another crucial dimension to the mission commitment so visible in the life of the congregation. As a congregation they have lived through many triumphs and tragedies together. Yet when Jim Borden, one of their pastors, was murdered at his summer home in 1984, the congregation as a whole was confronted by a tragedy of unusually personal dimensions. His assailant was a vagrant from another state, a drifter. Bill Lasher and his family attended church there at the time. Lasher says of those who were members in 1984, "They still deal with it. His memory's still there."

At the time people struggled to make sense out of what happened. One man says, "Jim was the ultimate good guy. I had nightmares. . . . It was almost like humanity's turning on Christ. This guy turned on Jim."[4]

Ten years later, those who knew Jim remember his ministry when the choir sings music he composed for them. Some know that the new organ installed in 1995 was one of Jim's dreams. Jane Turner Borden, his wife and the associate pastor at the time of his death, remained with the congregation as a co-pastor for nine years until she retired in 1994. She remains a part of the congregation, sings in the choir, and assists the pastors as needed.

After her husband was murdered, the bishop wanted to move Jane to another congregation, but she remained on the pastoral staff at the insistence of the congregation. Of this difficult time in her life she says, "I had so much good will. . . .This church protested to the bishop and they would not let him move me. The bishop really had to cave in. He didn't want to do it. He said I was too strong and nobody could come in and take over. . . .But they felt that they had to have me because of their grief and my grief, that we had to share that.

SHATTERED HOPE: SEEKING JUSTICE

Saratoga Springs has a history of leaders willing to engage the congregation in discussions of difficult issues, discussions that can lead to change for the congregation. People remember the consistent use of inclusive language in liturgy and hymns beginning in the late 1980s. But the use of inclusive language began with Robert Trost when the congregation was still in the "old building," and was continued by the pastors who followed him. Alayne Trombly, the director of music, introduced inclusive language in anthems, then in hymns, in the mid-1970s. People who joined the congregation then still talk about their surprise the first time they realized people were singing different words to hymns. The choir director told them that if they were distressed by the inclusive language of the hymns printed in the bulletin, they could sing the old familiar words from the hymnal if they wished. Resistance to change is regarded as normal and acceptable at Saratoga Springs and there are still people who express discomfort with inclusive language. But for most, the use of inclusive language in worship no longer seems odd or unusual. A new inclusive language hymnal, published in 1989, made singing inclusive language easier. Since then, the inclusive language policy practiced by the pastors has been introduced and explained in all new member classes.

The current staff and members of the Reconciling Congregation Task Force believe that the "struggle" over language laid the foundations for later studies of homosexuality. Nancy Law, who chaired the Church and Society Committee that planned and led some early studies of homosexuality in 1989, says there were "more strong feelings expressed, or heated expressions" around inclusive language than there were when the congregation later discussed the possibility of becoming a Reconciling Congregation.

Harold Smith, who chaired the Task Force that brought the inclusive mission statement to the congregation in 1995, says, "If they had not yet tackled the inclusive language issues, I don't think they would have made it. Some of the same buttons got pushed. This church had already battled that through for the most part. So, having gone through that, this [RCP membership] was just another justice issue."

It was Jane Borden who placed homosexuality before the congregation as an inclusivity issue. She preached her first sermon about homosexuality in 1988, and then another in 1989. After that she preached on the topic at least twice a year until she retired in 1994. She recalls that her repeated theme was, "They are your mothers, your fathers, your sisters, you brothers, your aunts, your uncles. Somebody in your family is gay."

Members of the congregation remember Jane's sermons, too, especially the point about family members. They also remember Bible studies when she led them in explorations of the passages that speak against homosexuality. Then they read passages about God's love for all people and explored the teachings of Jesus. Jane says her goal was to help people realize that "Yes, those words are there, but here is why they are not the only or most important teaching in the Bible. The idea was to be open."

It was also Jane who, in another Bible study series, helped participants realize that biblical language is sometimes literal, sometimes figurative. A man who participated in that study says that "part of her leadership, part of her theology, was to bring about a new way of looking at scriptures for many of us."

Jane Borden's ministry laid foundations for the educational events subsequently offered by the Reconciling Congregation Task Force in 1994 and 1995. Task Force members agreed to spend 1993 educating themselves about the issues involved in becoming a Reconciling Congregation so they could replicate similar learning experiences for the congregation.[5] This was their way of sensitizing themselves to the range of perspectives and feelings that would come to the surface as the congregation attempted to engage this difficult, emotional, and potentially explosive topic.

Among the studies they made available to members were four events sponsored jointly with a local Presbyterian/United Church of Christ congregation during Lent. The series included explorations of gender identity, a lesbian pastor who talked about coming out, a physician who discussed "What Is Gay and What Is Straight?" and a discussion of what it means for a congregation to be sexually inclusive. Later, a six-session Bible study was led by Camilla Smith, a professor of Biblical Studies, the wife of Harold Smith, and a member of the Task Force. The series was repeated twice, at different times, to give more people an opportunity to attend.

Task Force members were available for presentations on any of these topics for any organization in the congregation on request. They prepared themselves to discuss issues in neutral rather than judgmental ways, such as prefacing their remarks with phrases like "I have come to believe that . . .". They wrote articles for the church newsletter, bulletin items, and handouts for Sunday services. As part of a special effort to reach men in the congregation, Harold Smith led a Men's Retreat in reflection about the Bible and women's issues, inclusive language, and homosexuality.

During the years of congregational study, Task Force members were alert to opportunities to discuss issues related to homosexuality in their informal contacts with other members at church, in the community, and in their social life. They were especially concerned about the men of the congregation and concluded that since few men would attend their educational events, they would look for opportunities to discuss some of the issues in other venues.

There were many opportunities for members to consider the issues involved in becoming a Reconciling Congregation, through study, discussion, and in worship. A vivid memory for some was a sermon preached by Harold Smith in which he "burst into song." A Task Force member recalls that "He sang the Bloody Mary song . . . you have to be taught to hate . . . it was very powerful." The song from *South Pacific* says [actually sung by a young ensign and not the character Bloody Mary] "You have to be taught to hate all the people your relatives hate, before you're six or seven or eight."

After two years of preparatory study the Task Force submitted a mission statement to the Administrative Board. The Board approved the revised mission statement and recommended that it be sent for final approval to the Church Conference (annual congregational meeting) that would meet in January 1995. Meanwhile, Jane Borden retired in June 1994 and her co-pastor, Bob Long, received a new appointment. Borden, a key leader in moving the congregation toward inclusivity, retired eight months before the congregation approved the mission statement that is now on the Sunday bulletin.

Bill Lasher and David Vallelunga began their ministry in Saratoga Springs that summer. The Task Force met with them in October to describe their work to date. A Reconciling Congregation Program representative met with members of the congregation in both October and November to familiarize them with the nature of the new inclusive mission statement and to discuss membership in the program. Shortly before the January Church Conference, Bill Lasher preached a sermon, "Seeking God's Guidance Together," in which he defined inclusivity as "placing no conditions on admission to the family of God." His main point was that "for a Reconciling Congregation, the essence of the gospel is compassion not condemnation, inclusion not rejection."

The recommendation to join the Reconciling Congregation Program and to approve the newly revised inclusive mission statement, was approved by all but about a half dozen of the approximately 160 people who attended the Church Conference meeting. Although Bill Lasher and David Vallelunga were both very supportive of the work of the Task Force, David said later that the affirmative vote that night was a transformative experience for him.

> We had not been here that long and, judging from all the stuff flying around, on the faxways and such, it seemed like the vote, if not close, was certainly going to be strongly contested. I didn't really have a sense of the pulse of the congregation. And it was a very overwhelming night for me. I, in my own heart, kind of treasure the people. Because when we took a vote it was not even close. I was changed to have a greater share in the faith and confidence of the people and the integrity of their commitments.

During the years of preparatory study, very little opposition had been expressed to the exploration under way. Yet, on the night of the vote, television crews from local affiliates of ABC, CBS, and NBC showed up to cover the Church Conference meeting. Shortly before the vote there was an exchange in the local newspaper, *The Saratogian,* in which fundamentalists and conservative Christians from other congregations in town wrote "letters to the editor" intended to correct what they regarded as the congregation's faulty interpretation of scripture. Just before the vote, a woman from the congregation sent a fax to parents of Sunday school children saying that an affirmative vote would mean advocacy of homosexuality in the teaching programs. She had also contacted the radio and TV networks about the impending vote.

The sudden squall of opposition just days before the vote was the most painful thing that happened in a carefully planned process intended to give everyone in the congregation ample opportunity to learn about, discuss, and question the issues in advance. As Task Force members had anticipated, many members had not attended a Bible study or presentation about homosexuality or the Reconciling Congregation Program, but most had heard some of the sermons about homosexuality over a seven-year period, and they had been exposed to some of the same material through Sunday handouts and newsletter communications. There were about three families who were surprised to hear about the impending vote, including several Sunday school teachers who had missed worship services despite the fact that the Sunday morning schedule was arranged so teachers could attend worship. This handful of people, including the woman responsible for the last-minute fax campaign, subsequently left the congregation.[6]

Nancy Burdick, a substitute teacher who later said that she and her family were inactive and uninformed at the time, says the teachers who left were "dumbfounded" to learn that the pastoral staff was willing to perform covenant ceremonies or baptisms for gay couples. They regarded this as promoting homosexuality in opposition to scripture. The stated concern of the families who left—and the issue raised in the fax—was the effect of the new policy on children.

Nancy knew there was "education on different lifestyles," but says she had no idea that homosexuality was being "accepted by the congregation." As she looks back, she vows to never again be a "back-bencher." She admits that, at the time, she didn't want to be better informed about the congregation or have to worry about "the political end of it."

In retrospect, many more people left the congregation when it left the "old building" than the few who left when the congregation officially joined the Reconciling Congregation Program. Bill Lasher says the number of people at the Church Conference Meeting is not an accurate indication of support for the new inclusive mission statement. Many people considered a vote unnecessary, saying "We already welcome the full participation of all people," or "I thought we already decided that."

Although the night of the vote is a somewhat painful memory for some, in other ways the attention the opposition brought to the congregation was exciting, even affirming. As they looked out over the TV crews setting up their equipment, one of them quipped, "I guess we don't have to worry about how to get the news out to the community!" Task Force members and pastors remember the TV and press coverage with considerable satisfaction especially because of the spirit of the discussion preceding the vote. A Task Force member who spoke in favor of the recommendation that night said:

> The cameras were extremely intimidating. They were bright. Even the leading person who actually sent the fax stood up and said that she knew there were lots of opportunities in the past year or so for people to be involved in the discussion and learning but she didn't take advantage of that. Which I thought was a moment of graciousness, after all the things she did.

True to form for a congregation in the habit of reaching out to outsiders, the pastors welcomed their surprise visitors from the press and TV and members joked about their presence. As the Church Conference ended, someone said to the media people, "We gotta get you guys here next week!"

GROWING IN UNDERSTANDING

Every congregation that votes to become a Reconciling Congregation does so through some official process. At Saratoga Springs, the vote occurred at a Church Conference, the annual meeting at which new policies are presented to members for their consideration. This was the most democratic possibility, yet the affirmative vote of 160 of approximately 800 members actually represents only 20 percent of the membership at the time.

Bill Lasher describes the present congregation of almost 900 members with an average worship attendance of 400. Of those, an active core of about 200 to 225 people serve on committees that meet during the week. The others are "Sunday-only people" with a pattern of bi-weekly worship like that of many suburban congregations. But the "Sunday only people" are not just nominal members. Lasher says they support the congregation financially and are willing to trust administrative leadership to others.

Although educational events leading up to the vote were well publicized to the entire congregation, many of the people who participated in study and discussion of the issues belonged to one of two groups attended by the core of "active members." One of those groups is an adult Sunday school class led by Kenneth Bollerud, a high school chemistry teacher and the husband of Natalie Bollerud, the Christian education director since 1976.

The class attracts new members but many regular members have been members at Saratoga Springs for anywhere from ten to forty years. They are committed to serious examination of social issues and to Bible study. Class members have served as members of the Church and Society Committee, the Administrative Board, the Staff-Parish Committee, the Reconciling Congregation Program Task Force in the congregation and in Troy Conference, the Mission Committee, United Methodist Men and United Methodist Women. David Vallelunga says that "a lot of church leadership passes through that class, so that, in a sense, their study trickles down to the congregation." He also suggests that it is "a catalytic place in the formation of ethical thought."

The second core group consisted of several long-term active members who learned leadership skills at Troy Conference educational events about Reconciling Congregations. Several of them had attended Reconciling Congregation national convocations about the time the Church and Society Committee tested the waters with studies about homosexuality in 1989. They subsequently volunteered to serve on the Task Force of 1993–1995.

Harold Smith and his wife, Camilla, who led the Bible studies in 1993–1994, were relative newcomers in 1989. Harold was invited to chair the Task Force as someone who had clergy credentials and leadership skills but was not associated with the earlier studies of homosexuality in the congregation. The Task Force included a cross-section of members who volunteered their services.

Smith described them as a "wonderfully diverse group, not all of one mind." They made the decision to educate themselves so they would know and understand what is involved in being a Reconciling Congregation before they involved the congregation in the process. They wanted to avoid rushing the process, "cramming a vote through," or the perception that they were "working behind closed doors." Their sensitivity came from knowing that the intention of the homosexuality studies in 1989 was not clear to the congregation. The earlier attempt to introduce the Reconciling Congregation Program created some rumors and misunderstandings.

As Smith says, "We began to plan a program. And we invited everybody in on the process. We had speakers, some excellent films, discussions, presentations on scripture, the Bible, and the issue, everything we could think of. And we did that for two years."

Despite careful planning of the Task Force, congregational appropriation of the implications of becoming a Reconciling Congregation was hesitant and uneven. Task Force members say that trying to reach every member with educational efforts was more challenging than any opposition to becoming a Reconciling Congregation they could have had. Some church members still ask whether it is really necessary to include "sexual orientation" in the church mission statement.

Bill Lasher says that having a stated "open door policy" is necessary. "It's a way to push people's thinking by saying that our gay
and lesbian members are included in our open door policy." The
other reason to have a public mission statement—as he said in
his sermon the Sunday before the vote—is that "these are some
of the most oppressed people and so do feel the most unwelcome.
But we have to keep saying that, the reason why we had to push
the envelope to include by name these persons."

The pastors intentionally keep the meaning of the vote before
the congregation and explain the Reconciling Congregation
Program in all new member classes. They find that new people
are attracted to the congregation because of the open door policy, especially parents who want to rear their children in an inclusive congregation.

Yet in 1996 when they were interviewed, several Task Force
members wondered about the effect of the new commitment to
inclusivity across the congregation. One estimate suggested that
"maybe as much as 50 percent of the congregation is still very
uncomfortable with the issue. I think there are people who just
don't confront it. It doesn't involve them. They're not interested.
They don't pay attention. . . . And on a Sunday when we talk
about it, they wonder 'Why are we talking about this?' "

Bill Lasher suggests that "for 50 percent of the congregation
this is not a big issue. We are not a one-issue congregation.
Hospitality for all is a core value, mission is another, youth and
children's ministry another, music yet another—yet a commitment to inclusivity is an umbrella that covers all we do."

A year after the vote both pastors and Task Force members
wondered about how some members might react to the presence
of "people who were visually different in their behavior," like a
gay couple walking down the aisle on Sunday morning holding
hands. Since then, several lesbian couples have been received
into membership and their children baptized "without a single
negative comment."

Two years after the vote several people involved in the reconciling process expressed regret that the need to protect the identity of some gay and lesbian members in sensitive occupations

means they are not free to tell their story to the congregation. During their period of study, Task Force members had experienced the powerful witness of a respected leader who talked about being a lesbian Christian. Since then, some gay and lesbian members have openly witnessed to their faith, something few other laity at Saratoga Springs are willing to do.

Since then, former Task Force members have also learned that trust-building after becoming a Reconciling Congregation, like the preparation to make the decision, is also a long, gradual process. Some gay and lesbian members are still known only to the pastors and friends in the congregation. Others have joined the congregation as couples. More recently, several gay and lesbian members who had been attending alone for some time have been joined by their partners in worship.

Circumstances vary but anxiety about how the congregation would respond to gay and lesbian couples in worship proved unfounded. One couple started a Spirituality and Photography group that meets monthly. It has become increasingly apparent that gay and lesbian members recognize that they are welcome as full and equal participants in the congregation.

After the vote in 1995 the Task Force was dissolved and replaced by a standing committee of the congregation. By the fall of 1996 members of the new Reconciling Congregation Committee did not meet regularly and were unclear about their role. There was general agreement that it was a good idea to slow down so the congregation could catch up even as they would need to find ways to keep the purpose of being a Reconciling Congregation before the congregation. But they were not sure how to do that or what the next steps might be.

A possible next step suggested by various people was more attention to the education of children about sexuality and homosexuality. Another was finding a way to encourage self-disclosure by gay members and by parents of gay and lesbian children which they regarded as a big step for the congregation. As one of the Task Force members said, "In the sense of self-disclosure, we've never had it. And I think the committee needs to work on that for the future, that people can be overt about it and not feel threatened. But until they do, I think we have to be careful."

There is a Reconciling Congregation Program anniversary celebration in worship every January. In his sermon for the 1999 service, Lasher once again reminded the congregation about why they are a Reconciling Congregation, discussed same-sex unions and denominational "happenings" in the prior year. The Reconciling Congregation Committee was part of a group of six inclusive congregations committed to seeking social justice for homosexuals but sponsored no activities, other than the annual worship service, for the congregation. During 1999, 150 members of the congregation became individual members of the Reconciling Congregation Program.

As with the gradual increase in visibility of gay and lesbian members, the use of inclusive language about homosexuality has become more direct in the years since the vote. The intentional efforts of the Task Force to consistently use the word "homosexuality" during the two years of study made it possible to gradually move from references to "respect for diversity," "hospitality," being "reconciling," and being "welcoming" in general to using words like gay, lesbian, bisexual, and "transgender" in the printed bulletin as part of the call to worship or unison prayers.

Despite the actions of the 2000 General Conference to prohibit any congregation or conference from using the name of an "unofficial" movement like the Reconciling Congregation Program, the Saratoga Springs United Methodist Church continues to identify itself as a "Reconciling Congregation" in exterior signs, bulletins, and newsletter masthead. From their point of view, this action by an official body of the denomination only reinforces the need for a congregation committed to inclusivity as a core value.

BECOMING RECONCILING

The Saratoga Springs United Methodist Church is a congregation where members with different mission commitments have learned to respect those differences. There is a strong sense of loyalty to each other, a desire to do justice to the many mission interests of the congregation. For instance, the group that raised money for the new organ gave a tithe of the "organ money" to the mission budget. It is in this sense—wanting to "do justice" to the interests of others—that being a Reconciling Congregation is "just another justice issue."

During the two years of study, Task Force members agreed to talk about "reconciling" as a goal to be pursued, rather than "reconciled," as if the vote was the end of the process. In the years since the vote, there has been growing visibility of homosexual people in the congregation; parents are able to talk openly about their gay and lesbian children if they want to; gay and lesbian members feel good about their membership at Saratoga Springs. And, as Bill Lasher says, "Gay and lesbian members are no longer all anonymous." He adds, "We still have a way to go here."

Task Force members went out of their way to be "reconciling" with families who left after the vote. Even though they accepted the fact that these families had moved to other congregations where they are more comfortable with the theology, there is still a lingering sadness that anyone felt they had to leave.

Bill Lasher thinks that "the slow pace to becoming fully reconciling is the result of an intentional desire not to lose members and friends we care deeply about—to respect their understandings of faith and to continue dialogue on a level that does not alienate. To be truly an inclusive congregation one has to make room for even those who disagree with the majority. Some do leave the church and I consider it a failure on our part as much as theirs when that happens."

Due to the unusual history of tragedy at Saratoga Springs some of the "slow pace" he describes may be related to anxiety about violence. When members talk about conflict or tension they use stronger language than seems merited by actual events. Some think of the limited resistance to becoming a sexually inclusive congregation as having been "violent" when it was actually hidden and muted. There may have been only one outspoken opponent to sexual inclusivity during the entire learning process but several people remembered it as a threatening time. Jane Borden, the pastor who called on the unhappy member, says that the situation was not that serious. But a participant in the initial exploration of the Reconciling Congregation Program in 1989 recalls that there were several people who "took violent exception" to even talking about homosexuality.

His memory is that "this put a damper on the committee's aggressiveness to proceed with an agenda, where we were going to bring the matter to a vote." When asked about this, Borden explained that early in the process there were suspicions that a vote had already been taken.

Memories differ about what happened with the aborted attempt to explore the Reconciling Congregation Program led by the Committee of Church and Society in 1989. To some it was mysterious because the names of subcommittee members were never made public. It was mysterious to others because when meetings were announced, "the word homosexuality was not used at all. It left you wondering what it was. I'm not sure it could appeal to anybody in the congregation . . . had we been able to say 'This is about acceptance of homosexuals.' " Yet, it was also in 1988 and 1989 that Jane Borden preached sermons and led Bible studies that laid positive foundations for the later Task Force.

When the well-publicized and accurately named Task Force of volunteers was formed four years later, a deliberate effort was made to distance the pastors from being too identified with an agenda seeking sexual inclusivity. People point out that it was a good idea to recruit a Task Force chair who was not a member of the pastoral staff to take "any heat generated" because "we didn't want the lay leadership here to turn on the pastoral leadership."

While this concern for the pastoral staff is reasonable, there is also an element of protectiveness in the way people talk about Jane Borden's leadership over the years. Considering the fact that it was members of the congregation who opposed the bishop's plan to move her to another congregation after her husband was murdered, this is not surprising. The congregation has a significant spiritual bond with her, as she has with them. It is fairly unusual for a pastor to remain in a congregation after retirement. In this situation it makes sense.

There is a great deal of good will and appreciation for Jane, especially among those who shared her grief as she shared theirs. A relative newcomer who did not live through the tragedy with Jane and the congregation, suggests that there may have been "some undercurrent honoring of Jim Borden when we voted."

The memory of violence against a pastor was surely one factor in the affirmative vote for Reconciling Congregation membership at Saratoga Springs and may subtly inform attitudes of people who were members then. Natalie Bollerud, the Christian education director, puzzled over a lack of response by the parents of Sunday school children to sexuality education offered for children and their parents. In 1997 she said she had given up on trying to incorporate sexuality education into the Sunday school curriculum. The lack of response may not be too surprising, considering that the only objection to Reconciling Congregation Program membership aired in 1995 involved the parents of children in the Sunday school and was about the effect of congregational inclusivity on children. She says the congregation "doesn't want to ask judgmental questions. Ethical issues are something people really don't want to deal with."

David Vallelunga said that one of the reasons the congregation became reconciling was their implicit "theology of inclusion." He observes that this attitude comes both from the pulpit and from life experience. In interviews, several people who had gone through a divorce expressed gratitude for the nonjudgmental support they felt during that difficult time in their lives.

When he preached a sermon commemorating the first-year anniversary of the congregation's RCP membership, Vallelunga addressed continuing concern in the congregation about advocacy, noting that being a Reconciling Congregation "is advocacy but it's not specific advocacy. From the beginning of time, our advocacy has been for inclusion. So this is just one more way." From the beginning of the RCP movement in 1984, its leaders have made it clear that the goal of all Reconciling Congregations is not advocacy. Rather, it is "welcoming all persons, regardless

of sexual orientation, to participate fully in [the church's] congregational life."[7]

Discussion about becoming a Reconciling Congregation is a
time when members of a congregation are encouraged to break
the silence and talk about "sex" at church. It is generally
expected that these discussions will make it possible for people to
continue exploring issues related to human sexuality, which can
include some of "the most perplexing and painful choices in their
personal lives."[8] According to one RCP resource paper, when a
congregation is able to openly discuss heterosexuality and homosexuality, people "break the taboos and secrecy that have surrounded one of the most profound elements of human life."[9]

This may be an unrealistic expectation of a large diverse congregation where the commitment is to diversity of all kinds. A
respect for diversity at Saratoga Springs means that people
belong there for many reasons. Some are there for the music
program, others for the children's or youth programs, or the
fellowship and community. Some are there because of the RCP
membership, while others do not want to make an issue of it.
Bill Lasher points out that "for some who believe that homosexuality is a sin, but would quickly add that we are all sinners in
need of God's grace . . . why would we exclude some sinners and
not others?"

In Reconciling Congregation Program publications, "reconciling" is described as the bringing of both heterosexual and homosexual members to a fuller appreciation of all members of the
congregation regardless of "sexual orientation." At Saratoga
Springs this plays out as an honest inclusion of persons with different commitments, different orientations to the congregation,
and different theological and ethical convictions. In that spirit,
the congregation and the pastors are willing to learn what that
means as they continue their commitment to inclusiveness.

Jane Borden notes that the congregation has become even
more diverse since the Mission Statement was accepted. And of
herself she says, "I learned late in the process that I should have
carried a Bible and kept pointing to it as the revelation of God's
love for all people, not just some."

CHAPTER THREE

FOLLOWING A TRADITION: SEEKING A VISION

We don't listen to people, Lord, at least not most of the time,
Instead of true dialogue, We carry on parallel monologues.
I talk, My friend talks.
Remind us, Lord God, that you are trying to reach us both
In the miracle of dialogue.
Teach us to listen, Lord, and, in listening, to hear you. Amen.

At the base of California's San Gabriel Mountains, a church is nestled between rising foothills and the heavily traveled Foothill Boulevard (Route 66). The church is only partially visible from the road, marked by a sign and wide expanse of grass. Walking into the sanctuary, one's eyes are drawn to the chancel window, where people focus their attention each

Sunday morning on a panorama of foothills, mountains, rabbits, and trees. This congregation of almost 500 members thrives in a town with five colleges, two graduate schools, and three large retirement communities. At the town center, not far from Interstate 10, is a lively village where people gather to drink coffee, shop, or chat. A church and town of contrasts, both hover between busy movement and quiet repose. A church and town with traditions of social concern, both wrestle with issues of justice and quality of life. The 1980s and 1990s have, thus, been marked by the town's effort to slow environmental destruction by halting the development of undesignated, undeveloped land, and the church's choice to be a "Sanctuary Church," hosting political refugees in Our House, a shelter located on the church grounds. In 1993, Claremont United Methodist Church decided, also, to become a Reconciling Congregation. This is their story.

The prayer opening this chapter was frequently printed and spoken in Claremont United Methodist Church (CUMC) during the early 1990s as people wrestled with their decisions. The prayer expressed a yearning that people would listen well to one another. Earlier, the Claremont Church had spent two years in deciding to be a Sanctuary Church; they would spend ten or more years in deciding to be a Reconciling Congregation. This was a congregation that yearned for harmony but knew the anguish of families leaving; even the loss of three families during the Sanctuary decision signaled hurt. This was also a congregation committed to do justice and love kindness for all people. A tension between the pull toward inner harmony and the urgency of prophetic witness and outreaching kindness marked the tensions in the congregation during these decision-making years. The purpose of this study, as of others in this book, is to understand what such a community experiences as people decide to become a Reconciling Congregation, and then live with their choice.

During a two-year period the research team interviewed church members, observed church events, and studied minutes and other written documents from the past decade to try to understand what CUMC experienced in becoming a Reconciling

Congregation in May 1993 and as it lived the first few years of the new vision. The research team discovered old wounds and new hopes; we discovered the people's jubilation, frustration, and eagerness to live faithfully as a complex Reconciling Congregation. Hearing diverse stories of the congregation's history and present life, the research team analyzed and negotiated the accounts, emerging with the story that follows. The presentation focuses on the congregation's own emphases: its historical movements; educational processes; circles of interaction; central people and events; shifting emotions; and United Methodist connections. The chapter ends with interpretive conclusions.

THE HISTORY OF A DECISION

The church's lay leader introduced the history of the congregation saying, "This is a liberal church . . . it has a history to make a kind of social justice stance that is not always in the mainstream." Her words express what many others said as they recalled the historical events that set a course for Claremont United Methodist Church. The current pastor, Robert Davis, expressed his view as follows:

I am very grateful to Pierce Johnson [(the first pastor of CUMC)] for having put in print in 1963 that this is a liberal Protestant Christian congregation. When he used that word "liberal," that was a statement which apparently characterized the church at that time and set a direction. . . . He established a trajectory. . . . This church did not have a choice but to become a Reconciling Church because of that trajectory. . . . It became a Sanctuary Church; it had to become Reconciling. . . . Joining the Reconciling Congregation Program has been a crucial piece in the ongoing self-identity of this Congregation; it has many antecedents that date back almost to the inception of the church in 1957.

Whereas the Reverend Davis and his ministerial colleague, Rosemary Davis, rarely refer to the congregation as "liberal"

41

today, they do speak regularly of the courageous and warm leader-ship of the congregation and note the historic roots of the pres-ent community. A member experienced the congregation's tradition in regard to the reconciling process differently. He said, "This [decision to become a Reconciling Congregation] was an issue pushed by a special interest group. . . . It was hard-line liberals in our church." For others, it was not the automatic "trajectory" identified by the present pastor. One church leader encourages people to remember that the process was filled with "blood, sweat, and tears."

While opinions vary on the appropriateness and value of the reconciling decision itself, people seem nearly unanimous in rec-ognizing an historical movement. Some of the landmark events are described below in sequence. Of these events, some were con-ceived in advance, and others were simply responses to what had gone before.

- Beginning in the late 1960s, classes on human sexual-ity were regularly offered at CUMC. Lois Seifert, Martin Tucker, and others were involved in the educa-tional program on sexuality of the California-Pacific Annual Conference. As part of the frequent offerings at Claremont, therefore, weekend programs on Christianity and human sexuality were offered for youth and their families, continuing at two or three year intervals for most of the succeeding thirty years.
- In 1984, the Claremont chapter of Parents, Families and Friends of Lesbians, and Gays (PFLAG) was founded by CUMC member Lois Seifert. Since then, PFLAG has met there for fellowship, sharing, educa-tion classes, and events that draw members from inside and beyond the congregation. PFLAG still met in the church in 2003.
- In 1986 an openly gay couple started to attend the church regularly; then, some lesbian couples joined the church.

- In 1987 and 1988 the question of becoming a Reconciling Congregation was raised by some people involved in PFLAG; they had received information on the national Reconciling Congregation Program movement.
- By 1990, enough conversation was taking place in the congregation that the newly appointed pastor, Harry Pak, placed an Opinion Box in the church's narthex. Much of the visible conversation during the two years before and after Reverend Pak's arrival posed the real possibility of becoming a Reconciling Congregation; many of the Opinion Box comments expressed reluctance. One contributor raised a question commonly found in the Opinion Box: "Couldn't we accept everyone into the church as we have done in the past without making a formal statement?" Another said, "People of different colors and nationalities seem to feel comfortable in our church. Gays and lesbians must feel this way too since they are here, so why make a big declaration of it?" A strong objection was made by another contributor, who attached a clipping from the *Los Angeles Times* regarding unsafe sex in bath houses. This contributor wrote: "Five plus years from now, these same men will be angrily demanding that the rest of us provide care for them in their self-induced terminal illness; and that we find a cure for AIDS so they can continue such practices."
- In 1991 the Administrative Council decided to undertake a study of homosexuality. This study included a six-week study series, a resource and conversation table in the narthex, presentations to commissions, committees and other groups, and the mailing of what many referred to as "the little red book," a study booklet "On Becoming a Reconciling Congregation," to all members and constituents of CUMC (see appendix 2 for details). The booklet included statements and stories by church members and families of members. One

man, a minister, wrote, "Being gay within the Christian church stirs my memory of Jeremiah's deep experience of grief while serving God." He described the experience of being gay "as a recurring process of grief." A woman wrote of being invited by a friend to the CUMC after being excommunicated from the church of her childhood. She wrote: "A little more than a year after I had started attending services I became an official member. I figured I had been free-loading long enough. The minister opened the church service in which I was inducted by welcoming every-body to church regardless of color, income, sexual orientation. I remember shedding a tear or two of joy as I dashed home to catch the Dodger game on the radio. . . . Every Sunday I sign my name on the register pad, check the space indicating that I am indeed a member, and smile a secret smile. I have found a place where I can worship."

- In one other "little red book" story, a gay member described the difficulty his parents had in responding to him and his life partner. His parents first judged and then ignored his lifelong commitment, eventually set-tling for a loving, but awkward (and sometimes explo-sive) relationship with their son and his partner. The man concluded his story with a word to the congrega-tion: "A Reconciling Congregation would be a won-derful thing for parents like them. If parents could hear some positive things about homosexuals and their rela-tionships through the church, perhaps such families could be truly united and share and celebrate life's joys more fully. After all, if the church accepts us, why shouldn't they?"
- In April 1991, two months after the little red book was mailed, the Reconciling Committee (an informal group of volunteers) presented a preliminary Statement of Reconciliation to the Administrative Council.

- In July 1991, the Administrative Council decided to form a Consensus Seeking Group that was to represent viewpoints of the whole congregation. Their task was to determine and clarify areas of agreement and disagreement about CUMC's ministry to and with lesbians and gay men.
- In November 1992, the Consensus Seeking Group presented a report to the Council of Ministries[1] that listed six areas of agreement and five areas of disagreement. It was later shared with the congregation. Areas of agreement included the church's openness to consider qualified gays and lesbians as Sunday school and youth leaders, the importance of dialogue, a desire not to see anyone leave the church because of disagreement, recognition that "change is not easy," a desire to "make it known that CUMC welcomes everyone and ministers to the needs of all people" and a desire "to make it known that gay men and lesbians are welcome at CUMC." Areas of disagreement included a desire to declare CUMC a Reconciling Congregation listed in the national directory of RCP congregations, acceptance of the national policy of The United Methodist Church as stated in the *Book of Discipline* that declares homosexuality "incompatible with Christian teaching," rejection of the same *Discipline* statement; and a desire for CUMC to "be a prophetic witness to those who would condemn gays and lesbians." (See appendix 3 for the complete report of agreements and disagreements.)
- Using the work of the Consensus Seeking Group, the Reconciling Committee revised their preliminary Statement of Reconciliation.
- On December 15, 1992, the Council on Ministries adopted this revised statement as guidelines for ministry (see appendix 4).
- On January 7, 1993, pastor Harry Pak, Richard Bunce of the Council on Ministries, and Terry Givens of the

Reconciling Committee addressed the membership in a joint letter in which they reviewed the last two years and invited people to a public discussion of the revised Statement. This official church letter summarized steps that had been followed.

- On January 17, 1993, a special worship service focused on reconciliation, and Harry Pak preached a sermon describing his own journey toward reconciliation with gay brothers and sisters. He called the congregation to the importance of being perfected in love, concluding with these words: "There is an urgent need to come together in love, to share. Not all of us will draw the same conclusions. But that is not a reason to avoid the sharing. I will grow as I learn your reasons for concluding as you do. Perhaps you can grow as you learn my reasons too. As a church we can grow by becoming more and more open with one another. And that would be another small step toward perfection in love."

- Later on that same day, a Church Forum was held, and the congregation discussed the Statement of Reconciliation. According to a synopsis of comments, one divisive issue was the meaning of making a public statement in order to be listed in the national directory of the Reconciling Congregation Program. One person asked: "Why are we afraid to make a public statement if we do welcome all? We should be proud of it." Another asked, "What is the motivation behind making a public statement?" The chairperson described the National Directory of Reconciling Congregations, and someone added that a directory can be "used by people looking for a place to worship where they will be accepted for who they are." Another divisive issue had to do with the adequacy of the dialogue to date. One person said, "The UMC Discipline states that the church does not condone the practice of homosexuality. The dialogical process is important. Not everyone in the church has made the journey reconciling with the homosexual issue. It is still a divisive issue in this church and the greater United Methodist Church. To become an official Reconciling Congregation should be a longer-term process." Another person followed with a different view, calling the statement "a wonderful compromise." The congregational meeting concluded, not with agreement, but with prayer.

- In March 1993, the director of the national office of the Reconciling Congregation Program visited CUMC.
- On May 16 and May 23, 1993, two special Church Conferences preceded a week-long voting process. The agenda included spiritual centering, background regarding the process to date and the Reconciling Statement—including answers to frequently raised questions, silent prayer, discussion, and closing prayer. In the discussion, people spoke with passion and plainness. Gay and lesbian church members still recall the pain they experienced in hearing some of the statements, and the support they experienced in hearing others. Some heterosexual church members, empathizing with the pain, called gay and lesbian members during the following days to express concern and compassion for them.
- During the week of May 23-30, 1993, voting was done by secret ballot. People could submit their ballots before and after worship services on May 23; members who missed services that day were encouraged to come to the church and vote any day of the following week.
- On May 30, 1993, CUMC became a Reconciling Congregation. The vote had been on two matters: to adopt the Statement of Reconciliation (185 to 38, or 83 percent) and to register the church with the national directory of Reconciling Congregations (158 to 56, or 74 percent).
- After the long process, members of the congregation met the final decision with relief, exhilaration,

exhaustion, anger, and eagerness to move into a new phase of congregational life. A few families left the church, but the numbers are indeterminate. Some people say that "many" left; others say "three" or "seven"; others says "a few."

The present pastor believes that the congregation's history assured that the congregation would become reconciling, that it was "in the bloodstream of the congregation." What was this impulse in the congregation's bloodstream, and how was it nourished educationally? Other people place less emphasis on the historical trajectory, recognizing the sense of uncharted waters in which the congregation was navigating. To what extent were decisions shaped by the congregation's past, and to what extent did the congregation study, discern, discuss, and make a wholly new set of decisions?

Some of the educational processes described were obvious and intentional; others were more informal and unplanned. Among the planned events were the special studies in 1991, including the six-week study series on homosexuality, a resource and conversation table in the narthex, presentations to commissions, committees, and other groups within the church, the mailing of the red study booklet, "On Becoming a Reconciling Congregation," and some adult study classes. Interviewees especially remembered panels where gay people shared their stories, a traveling program presented by the Reconciling Congregations organization.

During the years, however, many people were aware of the quiet influence of simple moments, such as a gay couple lighting the Advent candles as a family during a Sunday morning service. These educational processes took place spontaneously as well as through careful planning, and they resulted in circles of interaction within the congregation.

In addition to the influence of its liberal history, the formal exploratory process and many informal influences in the congregation, Claremont belongs to the California-Pacific Annual Conference that has been actively engaged with issues like homosexuality and homophobia since 1982. Several Claremont members were familiar with Conference studies and resources and also provided leadership for Conference events.

In 1992 the Conference passed a resolution saying, "Therefore be it resolved that each congregation of this Annual Conference be encouraged to undertake a study of Christianity and homosexuality and to explore the possibility of becoming an agent of God's reconciling love in Jesus Christ by becoming a Reconciling Congregation."

We cannot say definitively how the congregation was influenced by its early, activist history; nor can we judge the influence of the various educational opportunities. Seemingly, all of these played a role, alongside the steady presence of gay and lesbian people, who soon became respected church members and close friends of many in the congregation. Gradually, also, families with gay members began to speak more openly about themselves, either in the congregation or in the safety of PFLAG meetings. The various educational opportunities provided safe places for people to gather information, hear stories, ask questions, share their lives, and consider different perspectives on human sexuality, and on homosexuality in particular.

CIRCLES OF INTERACTION

Before the vote was taken in the Claremont congregation, people had been gathering in many different circles for many reasons. The church was a veritable cauldron of people talking with one another, bubbling with their stories and opinions in the narthex after church services, as well as in organized circles of interaction. Some circles were planned to teach people, and some were formed for administrative purposes—to negotiate differences of perspective and to move toward decisions. Others were spontaneous. People simply wanted to spend time with like-minded folk or with people whose experience was similar to theirs. The circles of interaction grew from many sources— curiosity, eagerness to act, eagerness to slow down action or to resist a final process of voting, eagerness to find a safe church home for gay and lesbian people and their families, and anger over the reconciling movement. Whatever the sources, the circles provided a place where people could express their passions and hear the passions of others.

As people recall the groups now, they often speak fondly of a group in which they participated. The groups are named as critical places for sharing and being with each other. In many of the groups, people expressed themselves, shared their stories, heard stories that were like and different from each other, and tested an idea. Sometimes people actually changed their ideas, but almost always they nuanced and deepened their thinking. Whether the groups were structured or unstructured, they were almost always lively.

Some of the groups shared their ideas with the congregation. After a men's breakfast, for instance, one person wrote Harry Pak the sentiments of men at the breakfast. He said, "A concern that was voiced at that breakfast was that a formal vote on the matter would serve primarily to solidify positions, leading to divisiveness." These men understood their breakfast conversation as something of value for the larger community. Like the men's group, other groups felt that their gatherings were significant, that they could make a difference. We turn now to some of the more active circles of interaction, focusing first on formal committees and groups, and then, on other settings for discussion and decision making.

Among the committees and groups were the official Reconciling Committee, Consensus Seeking Project Group, Administrative Council and Council on Ministries. These each played a role. Each was a circle in itself, and the circles interlocked.

In the beginning the Reconciling Committee (RC) was not a structured group. Someone said, "Basically, it was open to anyone who cared to show up." The same person added, "There was a really strong attempt to involve the whole congregation. People from the committee were sent to each group and committee in the church to address the issue of homosexuality." The RC was eventually appointed by the Administrative Council to create a mission statement and then to revise it in light of the work of the Consensus Seeking Project Group. The group continues to this day, giving leadership to ministries with gay and lesbian persons within the congregation and beyond.

When many different points of view were expressed in the congregation, the Administrative Council appointed the Consensus Seeking Project Group to engage people with one another and to bring together a wide variety of perspectives regarding ministry with homosexual people. They were supposed to work together and find a common ground. Rich Jones was named as the facilitator of this group and their mission was stated as follows:

> To determine and clarify areas of agreement and disagreement about the core and peripheral issues of CUMC's ministry with gays and lesbians. The group is to gain a clearer understanding of each other's thoughts and to document the results of the process. The process and the results of it are to be shared with the congregation.

After some months of work, they presented a prioritized list of guidelines for ministry with gays and lesbians, along with the number of positive votes for each proposal. After a full year of work, they presented a final report, listing the six areas of agreement and the five areas of disagreement that were presented above. At least one church member (who later left the church) recalled that the Council of Ministries had focused on the agreements and neglected the disagreements. According to two interviewees, this misrepresentation and lack of attention to opposing perspectives caused alienation and finally led to the loss of members.

Alongside the two specially constituted committees, focused on the reconciling decision and on consensus building, were the ongoing administrative bodies. The Administrative Council, the major decision-making body of the church, advised a church wide study of homosexuality in 1991, received a preliminary Reconciliation Statement from the RC and subsequently recommended the formation of the Consensus Seeking Project. In short, the Administration Council was an active player at the beginning of the exploration and in the decision-making process, as well as in creating an avenue for negotiating differences within the congregation.

The Council of Ministries received the report of the Consensus Seeking group in November 1992 and adopted the revised Reconciliation Statement (revised by the RC in light of the Consensus Seeking Group's work) on December 15, 1992.

As questions and passions became more intense for the congregation, so did their discussions. What had begun as a few conversations here and there became a major topic of discussion at virtually every church gathering. People still carry vivid memories of these discussions, recalling them as significant experiences of the period of decision making. One interviewee said, "There was a panel discussion at our church one morning. . . . Gays and lesbians and their parents [whom Lois Seifert knew] talked about their lives and it was extremely moving. . . . It was the first time I really had heard people who were living it talk about it, and it moved from being a mystery to me to real, concrete, understandable."

Another interviewee recalled the strong efforts in the congregation to involve people in discussion. "There was a really strong attempt to involve the whole congregation. People from the RC were sent to each group and committee within the church to address the issue." In short, many discussions were intentionally planned, and they were quite influential in people's experiences and attitudes.

PEOPLE AND EVENTS

As questions and passions escalated, the role of significant people and events also became increasingly clear. Interviewees recalled again and again the influence of symbolic people, including both formal and informal leaders, and symbolic events, such as the vote. Their opinions of these leaders and events varied, but their symbolic power was broadly recognized.

Clearly, the person most frequently mentioned by interviewees was Lois Seifert. One person in the early years even submitted a letter addressed to "Mrs. Seifert" in the Opinion Box. The descriptions and evaluations of Lois's leadership differed according to people's views of the issues. One member, for instance, characterized her as "Mrs. Methodism [who] was a very committed person, who saw what she believed was right . . . and spared no effort to bring about change despite the cost of doing so." Another member said, "Lois Seifert was a key player. She brought up the idea of Reconciling Congregation, and a group of us started meeting to get the idea started." Yet another person, who was active in the early discussions and is still an active church leader, recalled Lois in this way: "If there was a head to the movement, she was it. I can't say enough about her, but she was the moving force behind everybody listening because she could listen to a person and then respond in a way that wasn't too hard to hear back."

Two other symbolic figures were Bill and Howard, the first openly gay couple to join the Claremont congregation. They sang in the choir and became well known in the congregation before most people realized that they were life partners. One member said of them, "They were—as an introduction to the people of the church—relatively easy for church members to accept. They were both devout Christians. They wanted badly to be part of a church. They had been raised in denominations which did not welcome them and that was a great hurt. They joined right into the choir. They are just a conventional couple, no wild hairstyles, nothing terribly countercultural. . . . That made things a little easier." On a similar note, another person said, "I saw people really warm up to the idea of committed relationships because we had some pretty good examples of that in our congregation."

Often mentioned by interviewees today, and often approached by passionate people during the early 1990s, Harry Pak arrived to be the senior pastor of Claremont United Methodist Church on July 1, 1990. He was aware of the discussions that had begun some time before, and he moved into the middle, intent on listening to everyone and helping the congregation reach consensus in their decision. When he realized that consensus would not be possible, he agreed to a formal vote.

Throughout the decision-making time, people with differing views on the reconciling question continued to appreciate Harry Pak's leadership. One person wrote to him a few hours after the crucial worship service on January 17, 1993, that "More than anything, I appreciate and celebrate your vision and leadership." Another person wrote in a similar vein a few days later, "We want to recognize your leadership in helping us build a church community which includes all people. You have worked hard to help us understand the meaning of love and acceptance for all our brothers and sisters. And you have taken risks in your personal and professional life to aid us in this journey. Thank you for being patient and caring and a model to us of the Good Shepherd."

Another person, a critic of the reconciling movement at CUMC, was also appreciative. "I am distressed that you have charge of a congregation administered by a group of gays, lesbians and ultra-liberal academics. That, however, does not affect my personal and affectionate regards for you as a warm and caring person."

During the same intense period of time, people involved in the reconciling leadership expressed empathy with Harry's difficult position. Two of them wrote the following in a letter. "We feel the need to tell you again how much we love and appreciate you. . . . Think of how much more smoothly your ministry at Claremont would have been if we hadn't come into that church and stirred up so much controversy! We are not apologizing! The issues needed to be confronted. . . . But we know that our presence and 'pushing' have made things most difficult for you at times. When people have been angry with us and at the changes we tried to make, instead of confronting us, they've dumped on you. We have caused you to be put in the middle between 'us' and 'them,' and that is a terrible place to be. Through it all, your gentle and loving spirit has been so evident. Your wisdom has shown forth. How blessed we at CUMC have been and are to have you as our pastor!"

The Reverend Pak continued to have a relationship with people whose opinions varied considerably, including those who eventually left the church. Leaders of the congregation often credit Harry, even today, for the spirit with which the reconciling decision was finally made. One said, "He was working very hard to keep everyone reconciled, despite the differences of all the people and opinions, and to keep them all focused on what they had in common rather on what they had in differences. . . . He did not want to have this a divisive thing, numbers of people leaving the church or feeling rejected." Another said, that he was "a wonderful, beautiful person, who was being pastor to every member of the congregation and was trying to be very, very fair to all sides."

THE VOTE

In addition to symbolic people, symbolic events were also involved in the reconciling decision process. The most frequently mentioned was, and is, "the vote." Accounts by interviewees differed greatly in regard to the timing and necessity of the vote. Church members who supported the idea to become a Reconciling Congregation approached the Reverend Pak and threatened to leave unless there was a vote soon. Others, like the Revered Pak himself, wanted to avoid the vote in order not to lose members. Some of the Consensus Seeking Group were also opposed to voting. One of them said, "We ought not to do it in this particular way. . . . If the congregation, the Reconciling Committee, insisted upon going ahead with this as a political issue, then they owed it to the church to do it over a long period of time." A member who left the congregation said of the Reconciling Committee, "These people were bent on making us a Reconciling Congregation. There was never any question whether or not this is something the congregation should do."

Despite the feelings of some that the time for a vote had come (or was past due) and by others that the vote was premature, the vote did take place. Looking back on the effect of the vote six years later, the new pastor (who replaced Harry Pak a year after the decision) said "the decision has been like a breath of fresh air." It created openness by officially welcoming gays and lesbians as well as created closure by ending the long, agonizing decision process.

In the years between the decision and the present, however, certain other events became significant symbols. Of particular note was the departure of some young families from the church and, over time, an increasing consciousness in the congregation that becoming a Reconciling Congregation needed to influence the congregation's ongoing ministry. Significant events since then include CUMC participation in the annual Claremont Gay Pride Parade Festival, a statement of welcome in the weekly bulletin and attempts to welcome people who left the congregation.

Harry Pak left the congregation a year after the reconciling decision was made. Some people assumed that this reaction was related to the process of becoming a Reconciling Congregation. One person said, "That wore him out." The new pastor, Robert Davis, came in July 1994. He immediately affirmed the reconciling decision and "went on with it," as one interviewee said. He also affirmed that the Reconciling Committee should not worry anymore about those who left, but rather respect their decision and move on with tasks at hand.

As life continues at CUMC, sermons or informal statements of welcome to all persons are shared in worship at least once a month. The Reconciling Committee continues to function, coordinating programs and reflecting on the church's ongoing work in relation to homosexuality. In the fall of 1997, an eight-week Sunday school class, "Claiming the Promise," involved fourteen people, about half gay and half straight.

Other studies include references to homosexuality as part of the larger subject matter. After the denomination's Judicial Council ruled in 1999 that a United Methodist congregation could no longer legally declare itself a Reconciling Congregation, the church reaffirmed its commitments in several ways. Even without the formal reconciling designation, the church continues to function as a Reconciling Congregation. When visitors open the weekly Sunday bulletin, they find welcoming words:

WE ARE GLAD YOU ARE HERE! Claremont United Methodist Church is a welcoming congregation and affirms its ministry with the whole family of God regardless of age, race, ethnic origin, gender, economic situation, marital status, or sexual orientation. Claremont United Methodist Church believes its diversity is a blessing through which persons are strengthened to serve.

Words about the welcoming ministry are also recorded in the *Yellow Pages* of Claremont's telephone directory. More significantly, the church continues to receive new people—gay, lesbian, bisexual, and transgendered—into membership.

One interviewee said that she believes the congregation as a whole is slowing down on the issue of homosexuality and returning to other issues. However, many new people have joined the church because of its stance and its welcoming spirit. A feature article was published in the *Los Angeles Times* in February 2000, underscoring the church's continuing commitment.[2] In that article, the congregation's minister of programs, Rosemary Davis, said, "No one is going to tell them [gay, lesbian, bisexual and transgendered people] or imply their sexual orientation is wrong, or that it is a sin. . . . It means we celebrate anniversaries of same-sex life partners with flowers on the altar and with prayers of thanksgiving. It means it's OK for a gay couple to come to the altar for communion holding hands. . . . They know that they are in a safe place."

In a church that continues active work in feeding hungry people and continues its ministry with refugees through the Refugee Resettlement Committee, homosexuality is no longer the central question, and decisions about homosexuality are no longer central events. Ministry with persons of all sexual orientations has simply become part of the ongoing life of Claremont UMC.

SHIFTING EMOTIONS

The present pastor sees a noticeable difference in Reconciling Congregations. Expressing his delight in being the pastor of

CUMC, Robert Davis describes the present spirit of the congregation.

> One couple drives about 45 minutes with their children because they want to be in a Reconciling Church, and they like this one. The father was active in their former church, but it was not reconciling. Another man from 30 miles away sought out a Reconciling Congregation, and he said to me, "There is a different feel when you go to a Reconciling Church." . . . This man is gay, and when he returned the second week, he came with his partner and a friend. They could not find a seat, and they walked down to the front. I was very pleased. The other family has no gay members, but they had been in a Reconciling Congregation before and they said they could see the difference. They are absolutely right. I see it too.

The pastor adds his own experience of the congregation. "I think that some people who were earlier opposed to the reconciling decision may have come around now, and they see this inclusiveness as a Christian teaching. All I know really is that the congregation took a vote, a plaque hangs in the narthex, and I have said, 'Let's go forward.' "

People, who have been in the congregation over the last decade, recall very large shifts in emotions. The interviewees name moments that provoked intense emotional responses. A lesbian member recalls the hostility she used to feel in some committees. "It's like sitting in hell . . . people are talking about how evil you are." Another lesbian woman recalls the days in 1991 when the red booklet was sent to the congregation. "After that, the heat started getting pretty hot."

During 1991–1992 when people threatened to leave if the vote was not taken, one woman said to Harry Pak, "I have already been informed by one very active and involved family at CUMC that they will be leaving the church over this Statement of Reconciliation. I had hoped that with care, correct information, and a dialogical process this could have been avoided."

Emotions were particularly strong for gay and lesbian members of the congregation. After a controversial church meeting, one gay couple was ready to leave. Receiving telephone calls from people who cared about them sustained them through that time. One explained that people started calling them, saying, "We want you to know that we are behind you."

This meeting was not the end, however. The Church Forum on January 17, 1993, stirred a lot of emotions as well. Some of the lesbian members recall how badly hurt they felt during and after that session. One of these women says, "We were compared to drug-addicts and prostitutes." The same woman was doubly concerned because "the way they said it was so mean and so hateful." At the same meeting, a father stood up and declared that it would be an abomination if the church allowed gays to come. He expressed concern that gay people would go to church camps and turn all the youth into gays.

That Forum was the last all-church deliberation before the vote; emotions were probably at their highest on that day. After the Forum, a synopsis of concerns was compiled, with comments by individual members. The strength of emotion was recorded also, but not in the synopsis; it was recorded inside people's hearts and lives. These emotions would be accessed much later through private conversations, moments of personal remembering, and the interview process connected with this study. At the time, many people were aware of the Reverend Pak's efforts to reach consensus.

People knew that young families were leaving the church but their reasons were never clear. One lay leader was sympathetic but a little mystified by the people who chose to leave. "They said they were unhappy with the process and had felt left out of the process of education and discussion, even though all the meetings were open and advertised." Another explained, "In my opinion, those who left probably would have left over another cause anyway." At the same time, one concerned person explained that the people who left "were thinking, sensate, considerate people who were driven off by the manner in which this was handled." The various views reveal something of the emotion that was stirred throughout the deliberation processes. That emotion remains a painful memory for many congregants.

CONTINUING CHALLENGES

What challenges the Claremont Church now? This is still an open question. At the beginning of the reconciling process, straight people were moved by hearing the stories of gays and lesbians and listening to their voices. In the course of our research we listened to people who were excited about the result of the process. We also encountered people who still feel hurt and some who left the church and joined other United Methodist congregations where they feel more compatible. One who chose to leave now says, "The congregation never knew how ugly it got. We were told that, if someone should leave, it should be heterosexual couples. The discernment process didn't work. Our voices were not heard." One family that left the congregation has since returned and resumed leadership positions. Another heterosexual person celebrates the joy of being in a congregation where people are free to be who they are. A gay man joins the church because this is the first time he has felt welcomed in a Christian church since he was a child. The voices are diverse, as are dreams for the future.

Ten years have passed since the final vote was taken to become a Reconciling Congregation. The congregation has increased markedly in diversity in those years, and its total membership has grown. Robert Davis, who is still the pastor there, sees a connection between the Reconciling Congregation decision and increasing growth and diversity in the congregation. He believes that the inclusiveness signaled by that decision extends far beyond sexual orientation. The decision tells all kinds of people that God's loving welcome is for them.

As the ten-year anniversary approaches, the Administrative Board, Council on Ministries, and other groups reflect on how their congregation includes some and excludes others. This means that children discuss inclusiveness ("accepting others" and "loving others") in their church school classes and they discuss conflicts when they emerge. Similarly, groups of youth and adults seek to embody inclusiveness in many forms and people continually discover new challenges and opportunities. Recently the church agreed to host an Alcoholics Anonymous (AA) group. When one of the AA leaders was investigating the church as a meeting place, he asked Robert Davis if it would make any difference that the group was a gay men's AA group. Bob was delighted to be able to explain that this would not be an issue because the congregation had clearly stated that it is inclusive.

In the ten years since voting to become a Reconciling Congregation, Claremont Church has celebrated their decision each year both on Reconciling Sunday and in many less formal celebrations in between. The people continue to ask themselves questions of accountability. Has the vote changed our hospitality, community life, and public witness? What more is to be done? How can we reach out to people alienated or hurt by the earlier process? What is God doing in the congregation today? Where is God leading the Claremont United Methodist Church?

CHAPTER FOUR

MAKING THE IMPLICIT EXPLICIT: THE FENCE AROUND HOSPITALITY

The salvation of this human world lies nowhere else than in the human heart, in the human power to reflect, in human humbleness, and in human responsibility.

—Vaclav Havel

The North United Methodist Church worships in an imposing gothic-renewal sanctuary located a short distance from "showcase" homes and the governor's mansion in a medium-sized midwestern city. The sanctuary and other buildings belonging to the congregation are situated on approximately three-quarters of a city block at the intersection of four U.S. census tracts. The two southern tracts house predominantly black residents. The two northern tracts are racially mixed. In the church's quadrant to the north, across the street, there is a city park.

The sanctuary was completed in 1931. As early as 1913 two of the city's leading businessmen convinced a newly appointed bishop to support their vision for a new church on the "north side" of the city. The bishop acquired the land now occupied by the congregation and recruited an Atlanta architect to design the basilican sanctuary of Briar Hill sandstone. He persuaded an existing Methodist Episcopal congregation, located 50 feet to the east, to merge with the newly formed congregation. When the sanctuary was built in 1931, there were 850 members. By 1943 there were 1,700 members. An educational unit was dedicated in 1951. According to church records, in the 1990s there were 1,100 members.

North has a reputation for a membership highly involved in congregational activities, as well as in the city that surrounds it. A self-study from the 1980s indicated that 57 percent of the membership was involved or partially involved, while the remaining 43 percent were highly involved and active. In the 1980s, after conversations with owners of small businesses in the neighborhood around the church, North purchased a large parcel of land on the northwest corner of the block that is now used for additional parking and businesses. Members worked with local businessmen to help stabilize the neighborhood after an unoccupied former grocery store became a problem.

In civic and ecumenical circles North is known for good preaching and a strong music program; pulpit, choirs, and organ remain front and center. Yet the congregation remains active in serving the immediate neighborhood. Various nonprofit groups rent weekday space, among them a co-op preschool and the League of Women Voters. Others are able to use the building for single meetings on request. In the spring of 2001, a "new ministry of community building" started a Farmer's Market with 16 participating vendors. This provides fresh, high quality produce in a neighborhood in which there is no major food market and where many residents have no transportation to shop elsewhere. The vendors accept government vouchers and food stamps.

An earlier neighborhood ministry from the 1980s began when several laywomen responded to a request from an elementary school principal looking for help with local children. The school's hot luncheon program had been canceled. Concern for "children's health" led the women to propose a program now known as "Bread and Bowl." The congregation still provides noon meals three days a week, year round, in co-operation with a local Presbyterian congregation responsible for the other days.

The self-study conducted in the mid-1980s resulted in a "Plan of Action toward 2000 A.D." Theological sections have been adapted for infrequent liturgical use. The "Role and Mission" statement remains in effect though "action" steps toward implementing the plan never were pursued seriously. In this congregation, where more than one-third of the members have earned degrees beyond the baccalaureate degree, there was no attempt to allow for the creative tension or empower the kind of leadership needed to implement a vision for congregational change.

Leaders who tried to introduce practices like systems thinking were unable to achieve a transition from a transactional to a transformational approach. In other words, the congregation founded by two businessmen and a bishop continues to achieve its goals through businesslike transactions.[1] The congregation has no lack of active members, experienced clergy, or financial resources. Approximately two dozen United Methodist ministers, one-half of them in retirement, and the current bishop's family are affiliated with the congregation. In 1996 the year-end financial report showed total revenues of $737,526.00 with $85,227 reported as mission benevolence beyond the congregation.

THE RECONCILING CONGREGATION TASK FORCE

In the fall of 1991 the Adult Education Council asked one of the associate pastors to teach an adult class on "Sexuality and the

Christian Faith." As the end of the series approached, many participants requested additional sessions. The group eventually brought a motion to the Administrative Board asking that a committee be appointed to prepare the congregation to consider Reconciling Congregation Program (RCP) membership. Action on the motion was deferred for a month because of bad weather. A month later, on March 18, the board agreed to establish "a task force to prepare the congregation to make a decision on becoming a Reconciling Congregation."

This was the third decade in a row that homosexuality had surfaced in a way that required a congregational decision. In 1978 an emerging church primarily of gay, lesbian, and transgendered Christians inquired about using North's building for worship and received a negative response. In the spring of 1987 several men and women affiliated with a group for lesbian and gay Methodists, were looking for a place for their monthly meetings, worship and other activities. The Social Concerns committee of the congregation was consulted and subsequently invited the congregation to join them in dialogue about the request from the group. The request was turned down, but in April of 1987 the Administrative Board authorized a Task Force to guide the congregation in a study of human sexuality. A year later the Task Force made six recommendations to the board including "ongoing dialogue within the church community."

After the Administrative Board authorized a Reconciling Congregation Task Force (RCTF) to prepare the congregation for a vote about the Reconciling Congregation Program, the board chair and the senior pastor invited six men and six women to serve on the Task Force. Members included a lawyer, a nurse, a professor, several business people, and the pastor's secretary. The group included a man who was retired and a woman near retirement, a woman who was divorced, a lesbian social worker, a gay educational administrator, and one spouse of a couple who had started a ministry with parents and friends of homosexuals. When the senior pastor invited a professor from a nearby seminary to serve as the RC Task Force chair, she agreed to serve as chair for one year.

Regular RCTF meetings began in the fall of 1992. The chair provided materials for members to begin to get acquainted with the Reconciling Congregation Program during the summer. After scheduling the best common monthly meeting time, two of the Reconciling Congregation Task Force members resigned due to schedule conflicts. They were not replaced. In all, the RCTF consisted of twelve people, including the chair and a staff liaison person, a diaconal educator, who met with the group. In time, working sessions were needed between full committee meetings.[3]

Educators use three adjectives to designate different layers of curricular learning: explicit, implicit, and null. The group decided that their topic, public inclusion of gay and lesbian members in the congregation, was an entangled implicit subject that would need to become spoken, explicit, and far less tangled. Their charge called for creating hospitable spaces for explicit communication on a subject that was nearly null in a congregation where most members probably preferred keeping it that way. Learning to communicate and be open to change began within the Task Force. Their own learning process guided them as they designed learning for the congregation. Several steps were taken toward more explicit yet hospitable communications.

Task Force members acknowledged that, if they were to respect each other as Christ's "friends," they would have to move beyond an "us/them" mentality. They needed to learn how to give space for differences to be expressed and received. Their goal for themselves was to understand and accept different perceptions, rather than unity, implied or explicit. Their fall meetings were devoted to this process. It was December before educational design became part of the conversation. In January, one of the members invited the Task Force, and the senior pastor and his wife, to his home for dinner before their regular meeting. At the close of the evening, as appreciations were expressed, it became apparent how far the group had come in moving from null to implicit to explicit.

During the winter the group designed a preliminary format for congregational learning in 1993–1994. The proposal included eight one-hour sessions—an information session to be followed by a dialogue time on four Sundays in the fall and four more in the new year. The teaching program would be scheduled during the church school hour, 9:45 A.M. to 10:45 A.M., between the two worship services. Dialogue time would be in the Fellowship Hall following the 11 A.M. service. There would be two sessions followed by three weeks of regular classes, then another two Reconciling Congregation Task Force sessions. The schedule was intended to avoid conflicts with the fall budget campaign, the launching of a building fund drive, and Advent and Lenten schedules. There were a total of seven teaching hours and eight dialogue sessions. Arrangements were made to videotape each of the teaching sessions in response to requests from church school teachers and choir members. During and after the series the videos were checked out. Some people arranged to come to the church to watch and discuss the videos together in small groups.[4] In the early spring the RCTF invited representatives from church school classes and other church groups to interact with them about the proposed format and to ask for a commitment from each group to participate in the sessions. The representatives agreed to ask their constituents to include the sessions in their class calendars. Only one group, the oldest seniors' class, chose not to participate as a group, though many of their members did attend.

Large groups need spaced rather than compressed time frames for learning. In conversation with national RCP leadership about the learning processes used in other large congregations, the Task Force learned that large, theologically diverse congregations often are involved for several or more years before attempting to make a decision. At the June, 1993 Administrative Board meeting, in her monthly report to the board, the Task Force chair requested and received an extension of the agreed upon one-year study to explore Reconciling Congregation Program membership at North.

As the Task Force planned for the Sunday learning sessions, they became aware of how rarely congregations choose to study a controversial subject. There appears to be an avoidance pattern when seeking biblical or theological reflection and dialogue about an issue on which members are likely to hold divergent views on topics. The staff liaison person and the Task Force chair shared this concern with the Adult Education Council early in 1993. In response, the Council offered a class in the spring using the book *When Christians Disagree* so there could be community reflection on social issues.[2] They hoped the class would help build a bridge into the implicit nature of the study to begin in the fall.

Early in 1993 the Task Force split into two working groups, one to create a study booklet for the congregation and the other, to plan the information and dialogue sessions. The first group prepared a sixteen page study booklet, "Shall We Become a Reconciling Congregation? A Booklet to Help Study the Question," which was approved by the Task Force. North's Task Force soon knew it was a poor choice of title because too many answered the title's question yes or no and did not go on to study the question. Copies of the booklet were distributed in June to every church family so members could prepare for the classes in the fall. The first copies were given to Administrative Board members. (See appendix 5 for an outline of the contents of the booklet.)

The second group planned the Sunday morning learning times, a series based on personal narrative and reflection. The goal was to assist congregational dialogue by encouraging people to talk about their own experience as gay and lesbian Christians, or as their friends and family members. The planners were careful to respect people invited to participate who chose to remain closeted. Fourteen people agreed to facilitate the luncheon dialogues. Eight to ten people were seated at each table with a facilitator. Two members of the congregation, one man and one woman, were moderators for the dialogues. The first and last dialogues were an hour longer than the other six forty-five minute sessions.

Eighteen people participated as leaders in the seven, one-hour information times. The Task Force wanted to avoid the impression that outside speakers had "answers" and intentionally invited only four nonmembers to be presenters. Two Task Force members who had different perspectives were among the leaders. Task Force members wanted to avoid appearing as if they were "in charge" of sessions, or "proponents" of the "whole affair" when they were not. They worked very hard to make it possible for the congregation to come to some understanding of the issues involved in the decision they would be asked to make.

INFORMATION SESSIONS AND DIALOGUE

On Christian Education Sunday, September 18, 1993, the senior pastor's sermon title was "Mission Reconciliation: But How?" The multilayered topic meant that:

> We shall have to listen carefully and to speak clearly and to hold the mind and the spirit open while the several dimensions of the dialogue unfold . . . and, indeed, the pastor asks that you give to yourselves and one another . . . it will not be helpful to foreshadow or foreclose that process by speaking as if we have all the truth now. It will not be helpful to withhold from one another what we deeply believe to be the truth. It will not be helpful to think we know that others should feel this or to withhold what we do feel. . . . Christian education is not indoctrination. It is not data transfer from the Pentateuch or St. Paul to the Saints of 1993. . . . Do not rule out the possibility that the God of us all will guide us in ways which none of us now sees.

The first information session on September 26 was introductory. Eight people explained how North had arrived at this point. In the hour and a half luncheon dialogue that followed, people were encouraged to share their hopes and fears. A form was provided for people to write down their comments and questions anonymously. They were encouraged to express whatever was important to them. The forms were collected, tabulated and used by the Task Force in continuing their planning process. The three remaining fall sessions addressed interpretations of sexuality from family, current biological and social science, and biblical perspectives. The style of the noon follow-up dialogues became slightly more confrontational as the groups continued to meet.

The Task Force felt that the sharing of personal journeys from North's congregation should not be introduced until the January 30, 1994, information session. The senior pastor commented on the experience in his weekly column in the church's newsletter, "North Notes":

> In a quite remarkable series of personal statements, members of five active North Church families shared their experiences in dealing with the realization of homosexual identity in their immediate families. . . . By the nature of the process some of the sessions deal with information and feeling "out there," third person references and "objective" discussion of the norm. This was not possible on January 30. Seven different voices representing more than twenty household members spoke in straightforward, earnest ways of dismay, fear, estrangement, pride, reconciliation, sadness, anger which have attended their faith and family journeys as a result of the phenomenon of sexual difference. It was apparent to all present that such statements were not easy to share. Yet, the narratives carried such grace and courage, yes, humor and pain, that all were moved beyond "talking about" to "feeling with." The deep gratitude of the congregation is due to those who helped us understand.

He continued:

> And gratitude also to many who have participated so attentively through the months. Well over 250 persons were in the Fellowship Hall for the presentation on January 30. More than 200 have been at each session. Approximately 100 have remained each Sunday for the 12:15 response and discussion periods. We still have much to do to find our way through to a shared response to questions clustering around this part of our human/faith experience. But we know now that we are not talking about some "them" nor about "data." We are talking about ourselves, our homes, our families, our faith. This kind of conversation is eminently worth sharing. And it belongs in "Sunday school," where people of faith wrestle with real life.

The Task Force did not meet during the months of the programs since the group had decided "to attend, listen, and contribute to the on-going process." A Task Force meeting was scheduled for March 9, prior to the March 16 Administrative Board meeting. The closing session scheduled for April 10 would be planned building on the preceding experiences. The Task Force chair met with the senior pastor on February 18 to discuss how best to inter-face with the Administrative Board concerning North's decision.

At the March 16 board meeting the Reconciling Congre-gation Task Force chair reported that people were not yet ready to choose between a deciding "yes" or "no" vote concerning Reconciling Congregation Program membership for the congre-gation. Task Force members sensed a willingness to continue fur-ther exploration of the dimensions of RCP membership. Part of the plan for the last session was to include time for people to complete a written survey with a variety of choices and also to express their own thoughts. Evaluation forms for the study booklet and the program series were also made available. The Task Force chair asked the board to take the following steps:

1) That the Administrative Board chair appoint a steer-ing committee of six people; three from the Board, one being the Chair of the Council on Ministries, and three from the RCTF. This group would meet twice with a staff delegate. A recommendation from the steering committee would be brought to the Adminis-trative Board for their consideration.
2) That a meeting of the Administrative Board would be called for April 27 to consider the recommendations. The Joint Steering Committee would mail these to Board and Task Force members not later than April 22.
3) That the current Reconciling Congregation Task Force, having fulfilled its task, be dissolved as of April 28, 1994.

The board approved the recommendations. The combined steering committee met twice. They received copies of the

Hopes, Fears, and Expectations survey plus three other instruments including an attitudinal response regarding North's ministry with gay men, lesbians, and their families and friends. The chair of the board forwarded nonconfidential correspondence. The senior pastor wrote a memorandum to the Joint Steering Committee that included two letters that had been sent to him with permission to share them. He referred to others he had received with confidentiality requests. He wrote: "The larger number of letters I have received expressed concern, anxiety, and, sometimes settled opposition to any changes of practice of North." He further expressed his own anticipation of pending requests for the use of the facilities and/or welcoming functions that might become matters for future decisions "if . . . thre [sic] is a general desire to be welcome and open to all." He hoped their recommendations would also address directions for the future.

VOICES, VOTES, AND TERMINATION

The Joint Steering Committee received thirteen letters related to Reconciling Congregation Program, nine negative and four positive. A document, "The Outcomes of the Work of the Reconciling Congregation Task Force, 1992–1994," was forwarded to the board on April 17th. Based on their interpretation of the Task Force's survey responses, the Committee drew up the following resolution: "Based on the evaluations of the study process, the combined task group recommends that North United Methodist Church should not undertake a decision concerning the Reconciling Congregation Program at this time."

The "Outcomes" document recommended adjusting the Mission Statement Flier to say that the congregation provides "diverse opportunities for worship, fellowship, and service, regardless of age, gender, sexual orientation, marital status, race, economic standing, educational status, physical ability, or any other characteristics which should not separate us from one another within the body of Christ." They commended "the Administrative Board, the Reconciling Congregation Task Force, and the church staff for their leadership and assistance through this process. God's guidance has been sought and valuable insights about important issues have been shared. We thank those involved, both for what has been done and the manner of the approach. Everyone deserves compliments, from the planners and cooks through the discussion participants."

The document continued, saying that "Based on the surveys taken in April 1994 at the end of the Reconciling Congregation Task Force process, it seems appropriate that North's study of how to become a fully Reconciling Congregation should continue intentionally. After one year, the Administrative Board should examine two questions: How well has the congregation followed through on these recommendations and suggestions? Should North UMC join the Reconciling Congregation Program?" The Steering Committee made the following program and policy suggestions:

- Invite Mark Bowman, Executive Director of the Reconciling Congregation Program, to speak here in order to identify the exact positions of the program.
- Confer with comparable congregations which have joined the Reconciling Congregation Program.
- Seek interaction with the gay and lesbian community and openly welcome their participation in church ministries.
- Encourage the Parents, Families and Friends of Lesbians and Gays (PFLAG) group.
- Let use of the church building, insofar as schedules allow, reflect our more inclusive mission statement.
- Schedule dialogue forums or other groups to continue conversation on this and other topics.
- Initiate further seminars for the study of sexuality as a good gift from God.
- Commission the Council on Ministries and the Commission on Education to create ways to use the new United Methodist curricular publications *Caught in the Crossfire* and *The Church Studies Homosexuality*.

As agreed, the Steering Committee reported to the Administrative Board on April 27. The following account comes from minutes of the meeting. The diaconal educator who was the staff liaison person to the RC Task Force spoke for the Steering Committee. She described North as "a loving, caring, inclusive faith community" and pointed out that the RCP study was undertaken at the request of the board. She described the "Outcomes" document as a "mid-course" exercise to continue the dialogue in positive ways and reiterated the recommendation that "no definite 'yes' or 'no' decision should be made now." She made the following motion: "Based on the evaluation of this study process, the combined task force recommends North UMC should not undertake a decision concerning the Reconciling Congregation Program at this time." The motion was seconded.

Before discussion of the motion could begin, an Administrative Board member stood up and said that as soon as the motion on the floor was voted on, he was prepared to support a motion that North Church not join RCP. He spoke as a member of the group that had worked for two years on the Role and Mission statement of the 1980s. He believed "the statement has served North well and will continue to do so." He was emphatic that North should not join the Reconciling Congregation Program and that the decision be made immediately, saying that "North Church already welcomes all people who want to worship here."

More than two dozen people who were present, some board members and some not, expressed a variety of views. A motion was made to table the motion on the floor—that North should not undertake a decision at this time—for the purpose of revision. The motion to table died for lack of a second. The question was called and a vote taken by a show of hands. There were nineteen votes in favor, sixteen opposed. The motion carried. The senior pastor voted with the minority.

Another board member rose and moved that the board submit a written request to the district superintendent to call for a Church Conference so the entire congregation could vote on whether or not North would join the Reconciling Congregation

Program. That motion was seconded. Asked to explain her reasoning, she said that the board was only a small part of the congregation and that this was a big decision for many, many people. In discussion of the motion, people spoke against membership in an outside organization. Others objected to a congregational vote to do what the UMC *Book of Discipline* delegates to the Administrative Board. The question was called and the motion for a called Church Conference was defeated.

The board was then informed that a request for a congregational meeting to vote on joining the RCP could still be submitted to the district superintendent by a petition with signatures of 10 percent of the membership (108 signatures). The minutes do not indicate who provided this information. However, as early as December 1992, this process had surfaced as a way to prevent North from becoming a RCP member congregation. It was advanced by persons who were concerned to keep North faithful to the "biblically based tradition."

A motion to mail the minutes of the board meeting to every member of North Church was made. The logistics involved were discussed and various opinions expressed. The motion passed and the senior pastor agreed to write a letter to accompany the mailing. In the letter to the congregation he stressed the fact that only one resolution was passed and it was that North Church should not undertake a decision concerning the Reconciling Congregation Program *at this time*. He also said that the congregation wished to affirm its mission statement of inclusiveness and welcome to all persons.

During the board discussion of the Steering Committee's "Outcomes" document, a member of the Trustees and Facilities Development Task Force was the primary spokesperson for those who wanted an immediate vote on a motion that North would not join the RCP program. Between the Wednesday night board meeting and the next Sunday the senior pastor and the outgoing and incoming chairs of the Administrative Board called a meeting of an "executive committee" of the board.[3]

On the following Sunday, May 1, the senior pastor's sermon was entitled, "What Holds the Church Together?" In the sermon he interpreted the majority "yes" vote at the Administrative Board meeting "not to undertake a decision concerning the RCP at this time" to mean "It is not the desire or will of the congregation to *join* the Reconciling Congregation Program." The two years of reflective learning, the survey outcomes, and the intentions of the Joint Committee for continuing study and dialogue were referred to as "that narrow spectrum question" and as an "over and done" issue. He went on to recommend the following three actions:

1) No revote . . . but to recommit ourselves to the broad inclusiveness which has marked this congregation and which I believe should continue to mark it. I think it is widely held.
2) Reestablish lines of communication and trust.
3) Celebrate the wonderful. Move on to other agendas of the church.

Operationally, the pastor's recommendation to "eschew" a revote meant, "Let well enough alone." From that Sunday on, at least two subgroups within North who opposed movement toward a public declaration of Reconciling Congregation membership had gained power over those committed to educating people for a decision that might have been transformative for the congregation. After that, those whose faith rests on a biblical interpretation that makes it necessary to reject as evil any form of homosexuality did not need a congregational vote to prohibit continued learning. Those who were committed to raising over three million dollars in pledges for the expansion and refurbishing of the church plant had won relief from a threat that could have jeopardized the building campaign. In so doing, they fenced in the extent to which the congregation would publicly proclaim its hospitality to all people for some time to come.

In June 1997 North's senior pastor retired from active ministry. He had come to North in 1974. His farewell sermon series addressed North's transition into the future. The next to last sermon was entitled "What Pastors Can and Cannot Do." For the first time in three years, there was explicit but veiled reference to the congregational interaction related to sexual orientation in 1992–1994. He referred to moments in his ministry as providing a daily invitation "to take in the direct goodness of God":

> So, for me, at least, the theological question is not the old problem of evil but the enigma of good. The real gifts of God lead to doxology and penitence—"how great thou art," "great is thy faithfulness" and "how broken and hesitant our follow-ing." And all this takes place in the imperfect venue we call "church." Where the priorities often move in divergent direc-tions, they change as we change, indeed, as we must as we go along. At times the word comes with intensity about the need for greater tenderness toward the environment and toward all creatures large and small. And then from another comes dis-may over societal cruelties and abandonment. And from oth-ers come patterns from the past that seem to be better than patterns of the present and are a kind of oral nostalgia which sometimes can be a drag on us. And others come with a pas-sion for particular companies of people who seemed to be excluded or pushed to the side. And others come with institu-tional anxieties. These are always present in the life of the institutional church, and they rise up, like Shakespeare's ghosts, to haunt us every now and then. Others come with visions so perfect of what might be that it is impossible to accommodate what really is, so beguiling that they make the imperfect present unacceptable. . . .
>
> Part of the legitimate necessity of the church is the diverg-ing viewpoints and priorities and words to share with one another and call to issue with one another. That is part of it. And, sometimes, if we are too idealistic, the pastor sees swirling currents and issues in denial, or disillusionment pours into this vortex of all these crosscurrents.
>
> So, what can pastors do? Well, we can try to live into the messiness of the church with eyes and ears open to the sur-prises of God's presence. Live in honest seeking to discern what God is trying to do. . . . But it is the task to keep at that question; that is not an optional language, lest the pastor becomes only a manager or a professional friend. . . . It is not

the task of the preacher to answer all those questions. He cannot. God has different words to give different people at different times. But the pastor can help us together inquire and pay attention to and find courage and joy in finding. . . . Pastors can help the church identify what it is it wants to be and what time it is in the life of the church.

Probably we overuse the language of our mission statement (of a dozen years ago now) about how mission grows out of our identity and out of where we are, our location—the crossing of those—to which I would add; it also grows out of *when* we are *where* we are.

Two such imperatives emerged in this congregation just a few years ago, as you know. Separate corners. One was to improve our facilities; the other to examine deeply our response of hospitality toward a particular group within our space in this city. The first has been virtually completed. For the church everywhere is wrestling with the question of "how can we be faithful to that hospitality which is universal?"[4]

HISTORY AS SYMBOL

Authors of congregational studies frequently reflect on the narratives of individual religious communities. Often a central self-understanding has come through some formative event in the history of the congregation, or is represented in some significant symbol, or is related to some respected voice of leadership. A central self-understanding can serve as a compass to help sort out faithful, future steps for the congregation. The "when" and "where" for North Church's story is rooted in its origins seventy years earlier when the businessmen and the bishop planted a new sanctuary and established a Methodist Church on the "north side" of the city.

The pastor's report to the Charge Conference, December 7, 1995, refers to a two-year process of planning and fund-raising that culminated in an October 15, 1995 celebration of having raised over $2.8 million. In 2001 the Administrative Board voted approval for an additional $500,000 to improve the landscaping and the parking areas and to renovate the sanctuary pipe organ and Steinway piano. At that time there was discussion about the possibility of building a fence around the church property. No fence was built.

Given the outcome of the process planned by the Reconciling Congregation Task Force, a question could be raised as to whether North should have undertaken an exploration of RCP membership. Was it a good idea to ask such a large, midwestern congregation to study homosexuality?

By 2002, the congregation continued to wrestle with the question posed in the 1997 farewell sermon of the longtime senior pastor. "How can we be faithful to that hospitality which is universal?" The answer is evolving in several ways. Implicitly and explicitly the subject of homosexuality remains.

The most notable event was the formation of "Leaven" after the decision not to pursue the Reconciling Congregation decision. It is a strong and growing support group for gays and lesbians that evolved from PFLAG (Parents, Families and Friends of Lesbians and Gays), which no longer exists. The group, which has a more clearly defined profile in the congregation than PFLAG did, chose the new name because it is biblical and symbolic. "Leaven" includes a regular Sunday morning class and scheduled social activities. Openly publicized invitations are extended to anyone who may choose to share in a class topic or participate in a special event. The group is included as a line item in the church budget.

In addition to the explicit activities of "Leaven" in the congregation, there is open and active participation of gays and lesbians on church committees and the Administrative Board. The terminology "gay" and "lesbian" is used in sermons. The Administrative Board supported a prayer vigil at the State House for gay and lesbian issues. Of this slowly evolving openness and recognition of gay and lesbian members, people say, "We are moving forward." Of the yearlong educational process undertaken by the Reconciling Congregation Task Force, they say, "We learned more about openness and diversity and how to make room for those who feel unwelcome."

In a lecture about leadership, Parker Palmer, the well-known author of books about how people learn, noted Vaclav Havel's words about the salvation of the world that lies "nowhere else but in the human heart." He added that Havel, the first president of the Czech Republic, was too polite to say it, but that our society's legacy also includes a belief that "matter is more powerful than consciousness."[5]

In the spring of 1991 the official board at North asked Christian educators in the congregation to take on the responsibility of consciousness-raising about how gay and lesbian members perceived and experienced an "implicit hospitality." At least a year before the congregation was to make a decision related to the possibility of becoming a Reconciling Congregation, actions were taken to halt the education program under way. The congregational learning at North designed by the Reconciling Congregation Task Force was intended to move inward into the human heart and downward into the realities of the lives of members and nonmembers. The discontinuation of intentional learning about different understandings of hospitality at North was a failure to take seriously the kind of spirituality necessary to engage adults in transformative learning.

In a three-part Vision Statement, dated 2001–2004, the phrase "Where Spiritual Journeys Meet" appears beside a picture of the cross that is the central symbol in the sanctuary. Continued spiritual growth in Christian faith does place the cross at the center of spiritual transformation. Those who plan adult education at North now and in the future will need to be aware that there may be a cross to carry when different spiritual journeys meet.

CHAPTER FIVE

TRANSFORMATIVE TEACHING AND LEARNING

A DYING CONGREGATION IS REBORN

Two stories told by members to visitors at Epworth United Methodist Church speak volumes about what the congregation represents. The first story comes from the mid-1960s. Concerned with a dwindling and aging membership, the congregation faced a life-effecting choice one Sunday. During the week a Filipino man walked by the church and saw the Methodist symbol; he recognized it: "That's my church!" On the next Sunday, Osias appeared for worship. When his family emigrated they came, too. Today Epworth is an ethnically diverse congregation that reflects its neighborhood because Osias and Francisca found a church home and became an integral part of the Epworth church family.

The second story that visitors hear is about a small group of older women. They met at the church one morning to work on a United Methodist Women's project. They walked to a nearby café for lunch and while there heard the gruesome story of a man freezing to death in a dumpster in the alley behind the church the night before. They went back to church, determined that if they could help it, people were not going to freeze to death while the church's gymnasium was empty. It was not easy to open a homeless shelter in Chicago; local politics and neighbors who didn't want "those folks" coming near were hard barriers to surmount.

For a time, church members were staying up all night to staff what has become an approved "warming center" for Chicago's homeless (warming centers do not provide hot meals every night). The shelter opened in the fall of 1986 and is known as one of the safest shelters in the city. Cuts in funding from the city forced Epworth to close the shelter one winter. On the first night the shelter should have been open, Pastor Bettye Mixon sat on the outside steps and told the men the congregation did care and would do all it could to reopen the shelter. She told them where they could find shelter; over and over, the men responded, "That's not a safe place. I'll just stay on the street."

Founded in 1889, Epworth United Methodist Church was a prestigious congregation in the once prosperous Edgewater neighborhood of Chicago. It is located only a few blocks from beautiful Lake Michigan, and the fieldstones used to construct this large edifice were brought by barge from Wisconsin. One of the few remaining signs of the congregation's prosperity is the endowed fund that keeps the fine pipe organ in good repair. Unfortunately the roof of the gymnasium, which houses neighborhood basketball teams and the homeless shelter, is not endowed!

As the neighborhood changed and many of its members moved out of the city, keeping up the large and aging building, with its lovely little chapel, inviting parlor with a wood-burning fireplace, many classrooms, gymnasium, and large sanctuary became increasingly difficult.

In the 1980s there was a pastor who told the small congregation that the church was dying. When they moved their worship into the small chapel because there was no heat and the sanctuary roof was leaking, he decided they should just "let it leak." About that time, two middle-aged sisters were looking for a church and visited Epworth. They liked what they found— friendly folks who were welcoming. When they told the pastor they wanted to join Epworth, he told them they were making a big mistake because the church was dying. Today, Joan, who is chair of the trustees, and her sister, Nancy, are a part of the congregation's backbone. They tutor, serve in the shelter, and give of their gifts in a multitude of ways.

This pastor was followed by one who loved the people, introduced inclusive language, and spent lots of time fixing the building. He modeled by his actions that this congregation did not have to die and that the building was worth an investment of both money and time. During his pastorate, the tutoring program for children in the neighborhood was begun by a committed laywoman, who also serves as organist and types the weekly bulletin. Epworth's tutoring program (preschool through high school) now serves over 125 children and youth each week. Some of the children from the tutoring program worship at Epworth on Sundays and many sing in the youth choirs. Tutors come from Epworth's small membership and from suburban schools and churches.

When this pastor was moved, after four and a half years of ministry, the time was ripe for church renewal. Bill White, who had retired as senior pastor of the Chicago Temple, the first Methodist church in Chicago, served as interim pastor from February to April 1990, when Bettye Mixon was appointed. Bill White's father had been a pastor at Epworth in the glorious past. Bill met with that group of folks huddled in the chapel because there was no heat in the sanctuary and said, "You have a choice. You can huddle in here and die; or you can open the front doors and be the church of Jesus Christ in this changing neighborhood!" When he retired for the second time, he helped the new pastor apply for funds from the Chicago Temple to do duct work so the boiler could heat the sanctuary.

And open the doors they did! Epworth members serve a meal each week at the shelter, give a party for the men in the warming center at Christmas, and struggle to keep the plumbing and heating working and to keep the roof from leaking in their aging building. It is not easy for this small congregation to keep up the building while they continue to open it to the community. However, they do so because that is their understanding of what good stewardship requires.

From 1989 until 1997 an Ethiopian congregation worshiped at Epworth on Sunday afternoons. In 1994, a gay charismatic congregation approached Epworth about holding services there. It is reported that at the Administrative Board meeting to consider this, one member said, "If we said no, it would only be because they are gay and that wouldn't be right." Another member said he was more worried about the "charismatic" part, but saying no because of that wouldn't be right, either. The congregation worshiped at Epworth for two years.

In October 1996, Epworth's initiative to address the needs of a growing Vietnamese population came to fruition when a Vietnamese congregation related to The United Methodist Church began worshiping at Epworth. When Epworth celebrated eucharist in March 1997 there were new communion trays on the altar alongside the congregation's bread and cup. Epworth's Pastor Bettye consecrated the elements for the Vietnamese service that afternoon because their pastor was not yet ordained. Bonds were formed as the two congregations shared the building. As the Vietnamese community moved further west, their congregation also moved west in 1999.

When Pastor Bettye came to Epworth, she brought a vision of God's "kindom" where all are welcome and where being disciples of Jesus Christ means engaging in "justice-love." It is a vision that recognizes the need to address personal problems and to work systemically to make the community and the world a better place. The pastor's work in community organizing prior to becoming a pastor was a gift she brought to Epworth.

Bettye's messages and columns in the quarterly newsletter, "Alleluia," encouraged the congregation to continue being a recognized "Rainbow Covenant" (mission-giving) church. She preached a gospel of inclusiveness. The congregation has had powerful celebrations of Children's Sabbath. Prayer time in worship always includes specific requests from the community for children, needs in the city and around the world, and for peace where violence reigns, for justice where persons are oppressed and victimized, for wholeness and health for those we know and for those known only to God. Lay liturgists assist in worship leadership every week. The pastor regularly shares the pulpit and table with members who are able and willing to preach and assist with celebrations of the Eucharist.

In 1992 a second-year seminary student from the University of Chicago Divinity School, Peter Jabin, became a field education student at Epworth. He was a gifted young man who was struggling with his own sexuality. During that year, the pastor at an Administrative Board meeting first raised the possibility of the congregation studying to become a Reconciling Congregation.

A gay couple began attending. They came from another UMC congregation that was largely gay and lesbian because they wanted a church with all kinds of individuals and families. A longtime member of the congregation became ill and confided in the pastor that he was bisexual and had AIDS. Just before his death, he allowed the pastor to tell the congregation. His wife stood by him and continued to worship and serve at Epworth until she remarried and moved out of the city. The congregation stood with them both.

In the fall of 1993 when my husband and I first visited Epworth, we found a congregation of 120 members—one-third Anglo, one-third African and African American, one-third Filipino—who were friendly and seemed to know and respect one another. At coffee hour, there was much mixing among the ages and races. The preaching was biblical and prophetic. All were included—from a homeless person or two to those with lots of formal education, from poor to not-so-poor, from children without parents present to families of every shape and description.

BECOMING A RECONCILING CONGREGATION

In interviews with Peter Jabin, the former field education student who continued as an active member at Epworth, and a young woman who was actively involved in the congregation through the 1990s, they agreed that, "It was never really a question of whether Epworth would become a Reconciling Congregation. That is the kind of faith community we are. The question was, 'How can we engage in a process that will be educative rather than confrontational and that will bring the most persons along?' "

By the fall of 1993 it was clear to the pastor and student intern that it was time to begin a process that could lead to Epworth becoming a Reconciling Congregation. A one-year formal process was developed as follows:

- Faith and Sexuality Series (three sessions in October 1993)
- Three outside speakers to lead forums on human sexuality issues
- An Annual Conference program staff person to explain the RCP process
- An open congregation forum (January 30, 1994)
- A follow-up meeting with the Conference staff person (March 29, 1994)
- Guest preacher Mark Bowman, RCP director, followed by a congregational forum (April 17, 1994)
- Exploring Homosexuality: Scripture and UMC Positions (May 15 and June 26, 1994)
- Guest preacher (Dick Tholin, Dean and Professor of Church and Society, Garrett-Evangelical Theological Seminary) followed by a congregational forum (July 17, 1994)

- Guest speakers (four gay and lesbian guests shared their journeys) and open forum (August 18, 1994)
- Open meeting prior to the vote (October 23, 1994)

While the schedule and topics suggest that the intent of the pastor and lay leadership was to lead Epworth toward becoming a Reconciling Congregation, there was also an openness in the exploratory process. Information from the Transforming Congregation movement committed to helping homosexuals be "healed" in order to be heterosexual was made available to those who wanted to read about an alternative approach to the issue.

Hard wrestling with Scripture was the name of the game. Persons with opposing views talked with one another. Because of the level of trust in the small congregation, people were generally able to disagree and to debate without choosing sides or feeling personally attacked.

There was also an informal, yet intentional, "educative plan" as Pastor Bettye trusted her intuition and her commitment to nurture, and as she challenged this congregation toward more fully embodying God's "kin-dom." As she reflected on her ways of pastoring during this time she recalled "pushing a boundary here, challenging an old assumption there."

She included the tradition of having a different family lead the lighting of the wreath during Advent—and she explained that the families would reflect the diversity of the congregation. Her introductions intentionally expanded our concept of family and recognized Epworth's diverse ways of " 'being family' together." Don and Alan, a gay couple, are a family; Diane and Terri, a widowed mother and daughter, are a family; a Filipino mother and father and their three children are a family; Eoline, Bertha, and Jake, three single women who live alone but care for and support one another, are a family. Epworth is a family and everyone is welcome.

Two openly gay men—who are called to ministry and have theological degrees—were invited to preach and "be in charge" whenever Pastor Bettye was away. When Bettye preached she was conscious of building on whichever of the lections challenged the readers and hearers of the Word toward inclusiveness, and she used these as sermon texts. When the account of the eunuch being baptized (a person judged to be sexually defective and therefore not acceptable to God) appeared as the lectionary reading, she invited Peter Jabin to preach even though she was present and led the service. When the passion story was read dramatically on Palm Sunday, she asked Peter to read the part of Jesus.

Pastor Bettye's commitment to providing opportunities for exposure and challenge in "soft" yet nonconfrontational ways helped the members of the congregation get to know and feel comfortable with gay and lesbian persons and to "remove some fears of the unknown." She hoped we could "live into this" without her needing to say, "See, the roof doesn't cave in and no bad theology is preached if we let 'them' be pastors!"

Finding ways to foster personal relationships and providing opportunities for gay and lesbian persons to use their gifts in our community led folks to see Don and Alan—not the "gay couple." It led us to see Peter as gifted preacher and one of us who loves and serves and has gifts for ministry—not as one who, as described in *The Book of Discipline of The United Methodist Church*, 1996, is "incompatible with the gospel."

Over and over again, the message was that Epworth is a congregation that "takes pride in saying we are diverse" and yet is a community united to accept everyone because Jesus Christ accepts and invites all to share the table of inclusive justice-love. God never intended folks to "be alike" or even to "think alike."

On the Sunday after the first vote, October 23, 1994, Pastor Bettye preached to a congregation in pain.

> At our annual Church Conference, we voted on the issue of becoming a Reconciling Congregation. In a meeting with 40 church members present, there were twenty-five yes votes and fifteen no votes. Because I had set two-thirds as the necessary number, the motion to join the reconciling program did not pass. The discussion around the issue was very difficult and there was a great deal of pain among every one of us in that

room. After that, it seemed to me that I could not simply pick up the assigned lectionary texts and go on as if nothing has happened to us as a community of faith, even though that would be more comfortable.

No matter what position we take, we all have this tendency to want to smooth the waters and protect the facade that things are normal, even though that is not always the way to health and growth. Anyway, that option was denied to me by the arrival this week of some pamphlets dealing with an entirely different subject. During one of the times when my mind was struggling with this sermon, I was also idly opening my mail. Just as I was asking myself if I should avoid this subject in this sermon, out of an envelope fell some pamphlets our Conference has asked us to distribute. The title is: "No More Silence—No More Tears." Now, I believe in signs from God, and rightly or wrongly, I took that as a sign—no more silence, no more tears. The subject of this sermon is struggle and the issue is unity.

The first Scripture text we read today [Genesis 32:24-30] is the story of Jacob wrestling with an angel. . . . You will remember that the struggle went on all night. Now, this was not your usual fist-fight with a winner and a loser. We are simply told that the struggle continued—and Jacob refused to let go— until he received a blessing from it. Keep that picture in your mind as we consider the Gospel text, Mark 4:35-41.

It tells the story of a storm that came up while Jesus and his disciples were out in a boat and how the disciples were terrified of dying in that storm, but Jesus said to them, "Why are you frightened? Have you no faith?" Keep that, too, in your mind. Along with Jacob's struggle that must somehow be turned into a blessing, add the very human fear we all experience in storms and disturbances.

The texts I chose today as New Testament readings are from letters by the apostle Paul (Romans 13:8-10; 14:1-8; 1 Corinthians 12:14-27), and in them, he tells us what he believes a community of Christ's followers should be like. There is "stuff" that makes Christ's church different from, say, the Rotary Club—and part of that "stuff" that identifies us as the body of Christ is that we are different from one another. [Paul says] that we should expect those differences, and yet, beyond differences we can and should find unity!

Perhaps we forget that in the early church, diversity was the norm. We take a certain sort of pride in our variety here at Epworth—and rightly so—for our kind of diversity is difficult to accomplish and mostly, churches segregate themselves into groups of people just like one another. But that wasn't the case in the early days of Christianity. People who heard Jesus and followed him and those who later listened to his disciples and became followers, were from all walks of life and all division of class and education. We tend to think the early Christians only had to struggle against being thrown into a lion's den, but the reality was that they had to wrestle with different backgrounds as well.

The early church was made up of Jewish converts, both those "high up" like Joseph of Arimathea and those at the "bottom," like formerly blind beggars and outcast women. There were those who had never paid much attention to any kind of religion before and there were those who sat in the high circles of the Temple. There were Gentiles and there were the Jews who hated them. There was at least one very wealthy woman who financed Paul's travels and there were those who hadn't a penny to their name. There were those who had no problem with eating meat sacrificed to idols and those who gagged at the thought of it. . . . And all those differences came together with nothing much in common except that some-where, somehow, a man called Jesus and his story had touched them and claimed their lives and their allegiance.

Now can't you just imagine a modern-day Administrative Board meeting with all those differences in one room trying to decide what to teach in Sunday school? But that is the audi-ence to which Paul writes—and it is another piece of the framework that I ask you to hold onto as we continue.

The true church of Jesus Christ [has] always been people of diversity set into the midst of struggle—trying to grab a bless-ing out of our wrestlings—all the time being tossed around in our tiny boat in an ocean of storms from inside as well as out-side. That's who we are, and that's who we are supposed to be. . . . [We must never] mistake our Lord's peace with comfort and lack of struggle. Don't ever mistake it with sameness in his followers.

Paul writes, "One believes this and another believes that, one eats, one abstains, one observes a holy day, one thinks all days are holy." That's not unusual—that's the way it is, but to be the Body of Christ, Jesus' followers must decide never to put a stumbling block or hindrance in the way of a brother or a sister. For the kingdom of God, Paul says, "doesn't have much to do with what you eat or drink or for that matter, with most of our human differences. The kingdom of God is righteousness and peace and joy in the Holy Spirit and the one who serves Christ in that way, despite any other difference . . . that one is acceptable to God."

I don't believe that Paul, in that passage, is asking any of us to simply melt into the mold of another's expectations. This is not a call for us to sacrifice our own understandings and beliefs on the altar of peace-keeping ——but it is a call for respect and for love.

There are honest and deep-felt differences among us as a congregation. . . . There are matters of conscience and matters of justice that each of us must struggle with. The words of Paul remind us that our devotion to Jesus Christ is measured by that struggle—will we stay with it until we receive a blessing? Or will we turn away because it is uncomfortable and demands that we engage one another, listen to one another and risk some pain? Will we lean on faith, and ride through the midst of the storm, or will we cry out to be spared its tossings and turnings?

We have not yet received a blessing from the struggles of last week—none of us—neither those who affirm the vote, nor those who regret it. None of us can call it a blessing until all of us can call it so—a blessing of understanding and unity over division and fear. I am not speaking here of peace at any price. . . .

I pray that we will have a commitment to wrestle until we receive a blessing in our differences and that we will welcome stormy waters with faith—and most of all, I pray that we will take as our pledge to the future: no more silence; no more tears!

A letter was sent to all Epworth members and friends from the Outreach Committee, dated December 7, 1995. This letter, written a little more than a year after the October 23, 1994 vote, picks up the story from the point of the first vote and brings us to the time of the second vote.

> For the past year and a half, the Epworth congregation has been in the process of considering what it might mean to participate in the Reconciling Congregation Program of the United Methodist Church. Although the vote taken at the Annual Church Conference in 1994 fell two votes short of the two-thirds majority set by our pastor (this was an arbitrary decision made by the pastor before the vote because she was concerned that we not make any decision that had the potential of alienating one of our three primary ethnic constituencies—her strong commitment to inclusivity made it necessary for the congregation to maintain its multi-cultural identity; this decision was agreed to by all persons participating in the process as a wise and necessary provision) a clear majority of the congregation did wish to join the Reconciling Congregation Program at that time. At this year's Annual Church Conference in November [1994], the Outreach Committee proposed that we again consider this question. A motion was passed to the effect that a special Charge Conference will be called early in February of 1996 in order that the congregation as a whole can vote upon the matter, and our District Superintendent has given her permission.
>
> Since the subject of Reconciling Congregations came up in 1994, we have had numerous study sessions, guest speakers, and discussion times to consider the issue. Leading up to the vote in February, there will be a few more opportunities for collective consideration. One such opportunity will be the presence of Mark Bowman, our neighbor and national director of the Reconciling Congregation Program, to preach and answer questions on January 14th. If you do not feel comfortable raising your concerns or questions in a group setting, there are a number of members who have volunteered to be available for individual conversations. Please seek them out.
>
> The Reconciling Congregation Program of The United Methodist Church is historically a movement on behalf of gay and lesbian persons within and outside the church. To be a

Reconciling Congregation means that we welcome gay and lesbian persons as children of God and brothers and sisters in Christ. This is, however, only one part of the meaning of being reconciling.

The core question of the Reconciling Congregation Program is whether or not the Church, as the Body of Christ, is open to all persons regardless of race, gender, economic status, or sexual orientation. When you vote on the question of becoming a Reconciling Congregation, you are not voting on whether you approve of homosexuality. You are not voting on whether you like homosexuality. The only question before you in the Reconciling Congregation vote is whether or not the Church will be open to all persons. The vote is not about sex; it is about justice.

To be a Reconciling Congregation also means to make a public statement to the effect that we are reconciling. We know that the method of making that public statement has been one of the concerns many of you have. It has been proposed that Epworth's public statement consist of: (1) modifying our brochure to state that Epworth is a Reconciling Congregation [with a brief explanation of what that means], and (2) affixing a small rainbow flag to our sign. The rainbow flag is chosen because the symbol of the rainbow is taken from the Judeo-Christian tradition. The rainbow symbolizes dedication to covenant relationship and the celebration of diversity. Part of the vote in February will be to affirm or revise this plan for our public statement. It must be understood, however, that the making of some public statement is part of the vote.

Please be part of the continuing conversation as well as part of the vote. If you have questions, now is the time to voice them. If you have comments, now is the time to express them.

After several more open forums, the proposed date in February 1996, arrived. After worship and coffee hour, the district superintendent called the Charge Conference to order for the purpose of voting yes or no to becoming a Reconciling Congregation. All members of the congregation were eligible to vote. The district superintendent stated the purpose for the meeting and asked if there were any questions or if anyone wanted to make a statement. No one spoke, so ballots were distributed and thirty-seven members of Epworth UMC cast their ballots. Some others who were present were not eligible to vote. They sang a hymn while ballots were counted. The report was given—thirty-four "yes"; three "no." They sang another hymn, prayed and the decision had been made.

After the vote, people wondered why many of the Filipino members did not stay for the meeting. By the next Sunday, when they were again present for worship, the other members began to realize that they had been given a great gift. The Filipino members may not have been able to vote yes, but they were not going to vote no either. They continued to participate fully in the life of the congregation as long as they continued to live in the neighborhood.

Despite the concerted effort of the pastor, the Outreach Committee, and other leaders in the church to foster open dialogue and to struggle toward consensus, four members left the congregation. One Filipino couple whose son had begun to attend a charismatic church and was extremely judgmental of Epworth's failure to "live by the Bible" left. One Anglo-American man who had been a longtime member and a strong supporter of the congregation felt he could not in conscience stay. One woman, who had joined Epworth in 1980, left before the second vote was taken. She wrote a long and thoughtful letter to the pastor but sent it as an open letter to many in the congregation. Near the end of that letter she wrote, "I've held my commitment to diversity and creativity in one hand and the Church's traditional understanding of sexuality in the other and wondered what to do. [My] journey has led me toward the healing of 'Transforming Congregations' and away from the accommodation of 'Reconciling Congregations.' "

While the RCP study and upcoming vote was not the only reason she stated for leaving her church home, it was clearly a catalyst. She concluded her letter, "I will miss my family at Epworth. But our paths are going in different directions and I must no longer delay."

The congregation grieved the loss of these four members even as they celebrated the gift their witness to inclusiveness was making and would make. They welcomed new members even as they grieved the loss of others.

TEACHING AND LEARNING EXPERIENCES IN WORSHIP

Much of the learning at Epworth occurs as the congregation worships and participates in fellowship together on Sunday morning. It is difficult for the small congregation to sustain a varied educational ministry or regular classes, especially for adults, due to the makeup and nature of the congregation. Pastor Bettye's sermons included unusual attention to interpretations of Scripture. When Peter, the former student pastor, preached, he challenged the congregation to recognize that there are conflicting teachings in the Bible. In one sermon he contrasted the story about the Ethiopian eunuch (Acts 8:26-40) with Old Testament teaching about eunuchs. He concluded by posing a choice. "With whom, then, shall we stand? We are given two scriptural models for dealing with eunuchs, for dealing with those who are seen to be sexually defective or peculiar individuals and we must choose. Shall we, like the Pharisees, stand with Leviticus and Deuteronomy? Shall we stand as punishers, as those who cast out, as wall-builders? Or shall we run, with Phillip, as fugitives and be willing to move beyond what our culture tells us is right and wrong?"

The sermon was very powerful, offering a new way to understand the story from Acts. It was preached by a gay man known to and respected by the congregation. Denied ordination by The United Methodist Church, he continued preaching as a member of the congregation.

The presence of the ministry of a gay man and several pivotal experiences began to define the congregation as inclusive before it ever considered joining the Reconciling Congregation Program. These experiences came most often during a lengthy period of congregational prayers in the Sunday service, a time when the pastor and lay liturgist came down from the chancel and stood by the first pew as congregants offered joys and concerns.

One Sunday, after Don and Alan returned from attending the funeral service for Don's father, Alan placed a small butterfly on the "Our Prayers Rise as Incense" banner used during Lent. During the community prayer time, Alan said, "Don's mother had one butterfly in the casket spray for each child, their spouse, and grandchild. She included me. I pinned mine on the prayer banner this morning."

Another Sunday, when the congregation arrived for worship, they discovered a beautiful basket of flowers in the sanctuary. The "birds of paradise" soaring above the arrangement were amazing. As they gathered, they looked at each other, wondering who died since no one in the prayer chain had been contacted. During the service, Pastor Bettye read a thank-you note from a man whose partner had died of AIDS. He wrote to thank the congregation for "trusting us to use your sanctuary for our memorial service." Both he and his partner had been raised in Methodist congregations but had left the church because the denomination taught that their love for each other "was not compatible with the gospel of Jesus Christ." For many in the congregation, the gracious thank-you note felt like a judgment and a challenge to work harder toward the kind of inclusive ministry modeled by Jesus.

Epworth's life together was never focused primarily on the Reconciling Congregation study and vote. During the one-year period of the educational and discernment process, Don and Alan volunteered to revive the rummage sale that the older women had reluctantly given up. The young adults and children from the tutoring program went downtown on the El to participate in Chicago's CROP walk to support international hunger-fighting agencies. Babies were born and baptized. The congregation rejoiced when baby Leah, born with one lung that did not develop normally, was able to leave her oxygen tank at home. New people visited and joined the Epworth family. People died. The choir grew. The children's choir sang at the Harold Washington Public Library, at Annual Conference, and at nearby nursing homes. They participated in a joint choir festival with other Chicago children's church choirs.

Fellowship time after church at Epworth is festive. Birthdays and anniversaries are celebrated at coffee hours. Whatever the age of the celebrant, singing "Happy Birthday" is a tradition. There may be cookies or cake, but almost always there are cheese curls. Sometimes there is Filipino fare; sometimes there are hot-dogs and chips.

Life together continued during the in-between time after the first vote. The Sunday following the first vote, Pastor Bettye's sermon set the tone for that time. During that year, the wife of the longtime member who had died of AIDS told the congregation that she "regretted not having shared that two of her children were also gay. It is something that to remain silent about may block us from including *all* when we say 'all are invited to the Table of our Lord.' "

After becoming a Reconciling Congregation, Epworth continued to attract new members, especially from among young couples moving into the neighborhood. As the local Filipino population moved farther west in the city, they were replaced by a Hispanic community, some of whom became members at Epworth. As they welcomed the Hispanic newcomers, they continued to reflect the diversity of their ever-changing neighborhood.

Some categorize congregations as either a "family church" or a "program church." Epworth has clearly been a "family church." They spend more time working, worshiping, and fellowshipping together than they do in study or in committee meetings doing institutional maintenance. During the week when members are at the church building, they are most often there to help at the shelter, or work on problems with the building.

When asked whether there was ever any doubt that Epworth would become a Reconciling Congregation, Joan and Nancy—the sisters who joined Epworth during the low ebb in congregational life in the 1980s—both said no. Nancy said, "I always felt the decision would be one of yes. We were ready to become inclusive in all aspects of our congregation. We are only follow-ing the teachings of Christ by becoming a Reconciling

Congregation." Joan said, "As we supported Peter for his ministry, I felt we must be supportive to him and others by voting yes. We could not say one thing and then do another. There were a few who wanted to stay put and not recognize the other side of the coin. It was a great feeling that we accepted them and all others and were able to become reconciling by an overwhelming vote. God moved many!"

EXPLORING THE MEANING OF RECONCILING

The witness and the struggle does not end with the vote to become a Reconciling Congregation. Epworth's diversity continues to bring challenges. There is not always agreement about what it means to be reconciling. For some, it is the central and most important ministry; for others, it is only one among several ministries in which the congregation is involved. Some members suggest revisiting what it means to be reconciling. Ernestine, an African American woman, said, "I was all for it and voted yes. I thought it meant including everyone. Now it seems like some want to make us a gay church. I was going to give up. But then a friend said, 'Why should you go? Stay and work. Welcome everyone.' And that is what I have decided to do." She helps organize meals for men in the shelter and is actively seeking to make Epworth a safe and hospitable place for all.

On May 2, 1999, when the congregation celebrated the third anniversary of the vote, Pastor Bettye was aware of continuing tension related to the fact that the growing congregation needed better ways to plan activities and make decisions. Some of the tensions in the congregation were about how to engage in the various ministries and how accountability is structured. She addressed this in her anniversary sermon.

> For fifty-two years, my great-uncle Jim was a Methodist preacher. He used to preach every year at our family reunion and I thought he was pretty cool. At one of those reunions, when I was ten years old, he asked me what I wanted to be

when I grew up. I answered, "A pastor, like you." Uncle Jim smiled at me and said, "Girls aren't pastors. Why don't you think about being a missionary or a teacher?"

Great-uncle Jim sent me a message that day and because I respected him, I heard that message and accepted it. What I heard was that my future was fenced in, limited, and restricted. He was the expert after all and, surely, he knew what I could or could not become. He didn't mean to diminish me by stating what seemed just a fact of life to him, but he did. I was forty years old before I broke down that fence, silenced the tape he had set playing in my head, and became a pastor—like Uncle Jim. . . .

This scripture from 1 Peter holds before us another voice, another evaluation of who we are and what we can be. The text challenges us to rewrite the bad-news narratives of our personal histories. It challenges us to take ourselves out of those internal prisons of fear and shame and walk into the true light of God's love and grace.

Today we are observing the third anniversary of Epworth's decision to claim the identity of a Reconciling Congregation. Many of you who came to this congregation after that decision may have questions about what we mean by it. Others may have assumptions about what it means. The truth is that, as a congregation, we have not been very clear about our corporate identity, except to declare that we are a place where all God's children are welcome. Like so many things around here now, this, too, needs some structure and definition.

Over the next few months, we will be discussing what we want it to mean and we will be asking all of you for your input because it is important for us to know who we are. This is especially so now, when our whole denomination is in turmoil and disagreement over the issue of homosexuality. The church has been in turmoil before—over the issue of race and slavery, over the issue of ordaining women. The church, if it is faithful, will always struggle with the question and who we are—who God calls us to be. . . .

The messages that tell us we are not worth much have been changed into the voice of Christ proclaiming that we are beloved children of the most high God. As Jesus was raised up from being the rejected one on the cross, so God raises up our rejected, crucified selves. God lays aside all the distorted, negative identities the world would lay upon us and calls us chosen and precious. And God calls us, as a holy people in this world. As people who have received a new identity, we are called to invite others into God's new people. In God's house, there are many rooms—there is a room for you and for me and for everyone. "Once we were not a people, but now we are God's people!" Amen.

In the May 1999 newsletter, Pastor Bettye invited the congregation to engage in some times of dialogue about the future of the congregation. In preparation for the first of these meetings, everyone was asked to review the congregation's mission statement:

> Epworth United Methodist is a family of followers of Jesus Christ. Founded in grace, united in support of each other, we share our faith through worship, study, prayer and action.
>
> Recognizing the violence and brokenness within our society and ourselves, we believe in the possibility of repentance, reconciliation, and change. We are called to speak out on issues of peace and justice, and to point the way of hope and healing for all who despair.
>
> Our commitment to our neighborhood is to be a compassionate advocate for children and youth, to serve the needs of the homeless, the elderly and the disenfranchised within and around us. We work with others to forge an open and caring, multicultural community.
>
> Respecting the differences created by age, race, gender, national origin, sexual orientation, social and economic condition, we affirm the presence and seek the participation of all persons regardless of these distinctions. Depending on God's grace ourselves, we seek to represent that grace to the world. We welcome all of God's children without reservation.
>
> (Adopted November 1995)

Between June 2000 and February 2001, the key leaders in Epworth's decision to become a Reconciling Congregation both left the congregation. In June 2000, Pastor Bettye was appointed to serve another urban congregation in Rockford, Illinois. And on February 21, 2001, Peter Jabin preached his farewell sermon. He and his partner were moving to Seattle. In a real sense, it was Peter's love, pain, and integrity as he struggled with his own identity and his call to ministry that became the catalyst that called Epworth to embark on its own journey toward inclusiveness. In the farewell sermon he expressed his deep appreciation for the congregation's role in his life and faith.

> I walked into this sanctuary nine years ago [as your new student pastor]. I had been told that either I would be scared to death and run away or I would never leave. I thank God that I chose the latter option. And in these nine years you have established me in a faith that shall not be moved all the days of my life. You have taught me what the church, as the Body of Christ, the Family of Faith, truly is. It is not an institution held and sustained by the clergy. It is a movement of the laity—just folks, who happen to be possessed of a vision of peace and compassion. It is a community that is willing to give its life that justice and love may be established. It is a place where children are welcomed and valued and taught and given hope—in order that they might know the promise of their own lives. It is a place where the homeless [the lepers of our age] are accepted and sheltered and fed—in order that they might know that they too are loved and included in God's promise. It is a place that will no longer be silent in the face of the abuse and neglect of God's gay and lesbian children, a place that will stand for and with us.
>
> You have taught me that this is what it means to claim Christ as my Savior, this is what it means to be the Church. And this gospel you have shared with me, I will share with the world wherever I go. . . .
>
> So as not to paint too rosy a picture, I must admit that there have been days when I thought Epworth was going to drive me over the edge. But even through the occasional burnout and frustration and conflict, you brought me to ever deeper understandings of the true nature of relationship and community and forgiveness and—hope. All of you have been my mothers and fathers in the faith—all of you. Even little Christina is my mother in the faith, for as she was baptized last Sunday she

taught me about faithfulness and hope as I beheld the wondering face of those who will carry on after we have run the race. I am grateful. . . .

This has been my mountain. Over and over again, this place, this community has been the site and vehicle of my transfiguration—my ongoing transformation into a disciple of Christ. My heart aches to say farewell to you—but it aches with joy, remembering the feeling of my own face shining because, here, I have beheld God.

The journey continues. There are problems to be solved and prayers to be prayed. There are interpersonal issues to address and pipes that always seem to leak into the most recently painted room. There are programs for tutoring children and their parents. The youth choir shares its witness in nursing homes and in churches. Work groups from other churches continue to come to help with the building and worship with the congregation.

It is not unusual for the finance committee to report a budget deficit because the hot water heater had to be replaced so the shelter could continue to offer safety and hospitality to homeless men. The choir continues to grow. The Word is faithfully proclaimed and all are invited to the welcome table of Jesus Christ.

A pastor leaves. A new pastor arrives. Members move away. New people visit. Some of them make Epworth their church home. Conflicts arise. The pastor and congregation try to address them in open and caring ways. All day Saturday brainstorming and planning meetings offer everyone a voice. Planning goes forward. As Epworth moves into the future, there is a need for some movement away from a loosely organized, highly informal "family church" toward more structure.

For this congregation in an ever changing and diverse neighborhood, there is no such thing as a status quo. But with biblical preaching, long periods of community prayer, a commitment to justice-love for all, energy that comes from celebrating differences, hard work, and a vision for the future, life at Epworth UMC is guaranteed to be exciting!

CHAPTER SIX

CREATING A NEW TRADITION: THE BROKEN MADE WHOLE

Come in, come in and sit down,
You are part of the family.
We are lost and we are found.
We are part of the family.

The strains of the opening song waft through the rooms and halls of a small building set off in a grassy lot on South Yale Avenue in Tulsa, Oklahoma. The location is on a main artery and busy traffic route in the area known as midtown. It is surrounded by modest residential housing with Interstate 244 several miles north, businesses, several churches, and a branch of the University of Oklahoma School of Medicine located near the intersection of an expressway to the south and a large mall several miles on down the thoroughfare.

It is 6:00 P.M. on a rainy Sunday evening in early September 1998; the central time of celebration and worship has begun for the sixty-plus persons who have gathered in the large rectangular room designated as the celebration center. The room is arranged to face the widest wall, with folding chairs placed in rows of semi-circles around a table in the center. On the side opposite the entrance, the wall is covered with a giant mural of many colored handprints; some solid, some splattered, some two-toned, connected in random fashion. Banners and pictures have been placed on other walls around the room.

> *You know the reason why you came*
> *Yet no reason can explain*
> *So share in the laughter, and cry in the pain,*
> *For we are part of the family.*

Evidence of repair in progress can be seen around the room, some flaking paint, a lead stain, and several missing tiles in the ceiling, while newly installed flush fluorescent lighting fixtures brighten the space. The sound system is in place picking up the tones from the piano and catching the leader's voice. In the early spring this space became the fourth location of Community of Hope. For the fourth time the community is refurbishing space in which it can meet. Latecomers find their way to empty chairs greeted by extended hands, smiles, and voiced welcomes. The group is diverse in age, dominantly white, dressed casually in jeans, shorts, tees, skirts, and slacks. Outside a freshly painted and lettered sign has been placed near landscaped shrubs and flowers: Community of Hope United Methodist Shalom Base Community.

> *Children and elders, middlers and teens,*
> *Singles and doubles and in-betweens,*
> *Folks of all colors, gay, straight, large and lean,*
> *We're all a part of the family.*

As the song is finished, the leader lifts a candle in rainbow hues off the central table and proclaims, "Lighting this candle is our witness that in all things, we have chosen to hope rather than to curse the darkness." The group responds, "We live in God's world. We are called to be God's people. In life, in death, in life beyond death, we are not alone." Only those who are a part of this group would know that this affirmation was made by persons of all sexual orientations, drug addicted and alcoholic, incarcerated, homeless, educated, unemployed, single, married, divorced, and coupled, churched and unchurched. These are the companions and visitors of Community of Hope, who have gathered to hear the Word in Scripture and witness, to sing hymns, to join in prayer, to voice joys and concerns, to announce mission projects, to receive the bread and wine, and to be sent out to serve as God's forgiven and reconciled people.[1]

The service ends as all form a circle around the room and sing together:

> Shalom to you now, shalom my friends;
> May God's full mercies bless you, my friends.
> In all your living and through your loving,
> Christ be your shalom, Christ be your shalom.

THE SHALOM BASE COMMUNITY

Over the span of several years, a large United Methodist church in Tulsa had developed a fledgling ministry to people regarded as on the fringes of society, especially people suffering with HIV/AIDS. The ministry developed largely due to the efforts of the associate pastor who had previously served the church as a lay employee, and during her seminary years, as the youth minister. During the four years that the associate pastor was appointed to the position of Minister of Discipleship, the ministry expanded. This led to acquaintance, work, and friendship with gay and lesbian individuals and couples who were welcomed to the church. These people brought a new profile to a congregation whose membership had been composed of straight, predominantly white, middle-class, blue-collar families who lived in the suburbs that had sprung up on the east side of Tulsa. Over time, several people from the gay community joined the church and became quite active under the associate pastor's leadership, and with support and involvement from the senior pastor, other staff members and members of the congregation.

The adult Sunday school class named "Micah 6:8" had become quite involved in several social justice projects in response to the Bible study in which they were engaged. The class, led by the associate pastor, had attracted several dozen adults in the congregation who were interested in exploring the margins of society as a place of ministry. Some persons outside the congregation that members had met through these projects were invited to attend the class. Several persons began to attend regularly, taking part in worship and other activities of the congregation, and eventually joining the church.

In preparation for being informed about deliberations of the 1992 General Conference, a series of four seminars was planned for the congregation and offered by the pastors focusing on pertinent issues that were to be debated at the conference: the pension plan, baptism, homosexuality, and abortion. Some division and friction occurred in the church as a result of persons' responses to the seminars and heightened as The United Methodist Church finalized its positions at General Conference.

Friction increased among the members and discontent with the ministry of the associate pastor was expressed by a significant number of the congregation. The friction and discontent were fueled by several issues among which were the following: the associate pastor's open support of homosexuality as an alternative lifestyle, the decision reached by the General Conference on homosexuality, the baptism of two men who were openly known as a gay couple, and the policy of the congregation that no one who was sick or diseased could be invited to assist the elders in the distribution of the communion elements. There were rumblings of private meetings being conducted in homes to discuss the termination of the associate pastor.

During some of this same period, the church struggled with meeting the budget. Eventually, a financial crisis occurred, resulting in a recommendation by the finance committee that significant cuts should be made; the budget for several programs was reduced and several staff positions were eliminated. The position of associate pastor was one of those eliminated for the next year. Thereby, the church did not request the appointment of an associate pastor for the ensuing year.

Preceding Annual Conference, the associate pastor continued to work with the strongly committed group that had emerged out of the "Micah 6:8" Sunday school class. They spent special time studying the parables and the "reign of God." The parable of the mustard seed, a weed growing prolifically, became their dominant image as they attempted to discern what shape ministry would take for them. During that time they determined that they could not continue to exist at the large United Methodist church. They invited the district superintendent to talk with them about a vision of a new community.[2] They began to work with the district superintendent and the associate pastor about possible goals for this new community.

Prior to this time the associate pastor had led several mission teams to Central America and had participated in the life of several Base Communities in Nicaragua. She had also participated in the Shalom Zone initiative of The United Methodist Church. Her focus in ministry was developing around a call to minister with the oppressed and the marginalized. When she learned that she would be asked to leave the large United Methodist church, the associate pastor requested a meeting with the bishop of the Oklahoma Annual Conference. She recalled: "I requested a visit with [the] bishop . . . to discuss my hopes and dreams for ministry and my fears about several marginalized communities within Tulsa that were at risk of being left with little or no pastoral presence or care——the HIV/AIDS community, the 'recovery' community, women dealing with poverty and abuse, and the gay and lesbian community. After several months of dreaming, wondering, researching, political jockeying, and praying, we hit upon the idea of a 'base community' approach."

The bishop had just returned from Central America where he had what he later described in an address to the Tulsa District as a "life changing" experience. His experience in Central America reinforced impressions formed during study at the Oxford Methodist Institute earlier that summer. At that time, the model of "shalom communities," communities committed to ministries of healing, support, and empowerment, was being developed in the UMC. The bishop and associate pastor began to explore the possibility of combining the model of "shalom communities" with the "base community" model from Latin America. "Neither one of us had a clear sense of what that might be, but the agreed upon emphasis was ministry to and with those who were socially, religiously, and economically marginalized." The bishop worked with his cabinet to secure $12,000 in salary support and the pastor agreed to accept a "less than full-time" appointment in which she would have the freedom to explore how the base community model might take shape in Tulsa. At the 1993 session of Annual Conference, the bishop announced that a Shalom Base Community was starting in Tulsa. The appointment of a pastor was made and included in the official printed list of appointments distributed during the final session of Annual Conference.

The pastor began her new work by inviting thirteen people to become the core group of this base community; most of them had been a part of the "Micah 6:8" class. "That initial group consisted of three heterosexual families with children, a lesbian couple with children, a gay couple both of whom had AIDS, and two single gay men, and . . . our district superintendent." This group did the initial planning and visioning. Out of their early work together they began to know that it would be critical to create a balance between hospitality within and outreach beyond the community, as well as the importance of celebrating diversity. From the beginning there was a commitment to fight racism, sexism, classism, and homophobia based on the scripture, "What does the LORD require of you but to do justice, and to love kindness, and to walk humbly with your God?" (Micah 6:8). A mission statement began to take shape and the group was able to articulate a consensus:

> We are a United Methodist congregation who understand our mission to be; to respond faithfully to God's unconditional love by living as an intentionally multicultural, inclusive community that seeks, welcomes, and values all people. And to act as the living Body of Christ by seeking justice, compassion, and liberation with and for those whom our society has marginalized.

Scriptures undergirding the group that became the focus and theme for several Bible studies led by the pastor were Jeremiah 29:1-11—"seek the welfare of the city where I have sent you into exile"; Mark 4:35-40—"he said to them, 'Let us go across to the other side' "; and 2 Corinthians 5:16-20—"we are ambassadors for Christ." In light of the mission statement they agreed that the organizational structure of the community was to be nonhierarchical and team oriented with collaborative decision making and needs-based organizational style. They saw themselves to be both a community of shalom and a community working for shalom.

Once the mission was articulated, ideas for naming the community began to surface. Inspired by the vision they had found together in the ancient Scripture and excited by the possibility of a different way of being a church, the founding group gathered early in May 1993, in the living room of the pastor's home. Out of their talking and listening and wrestling together about "God's hope for a new community in this time and this place," the name Community of Hope was chosen. The pastor recalls: "At the same time, [the] bishop . . . was publishing the name of this new mission as 'Shalom Base Community.' And thus it was that in June of 1993, the Tulsa district superintendent and I drove to North Tulsa to the only African American owned bank in Tulsa to open a checking account in the name of the 'United Methodist Community of Hope Shalom Base Community.' " The money to open this account was a $300 gift to the pastor for conducting the funeral of a person who had died of AIDS. There was no church building, no office, no telephone, no supplies, and no official connection to the Conference structure.

Working out of a storage room in the office of one of the group, a letter was sent to various people, churches, and organizations in Tulsa inviting them to attend and support the first official gathering of the United Methodist Community of Hope Shalom Base Community (COH). A place to meet had been negotiated and the first official gathering of the new community took place in the basement of another United Methodist church, Tulsa, on June 20, 1993, at 6:30 P.M. with more than forty people present to worship and celebrate.

At the worship service that evening the first Rainbow Christ Candle was lit. As preparation for communion was made, a member of the founding group gave the community a chalice he had found while attending the International AIDS Conference in Germany—a broken-yet-made-whole chalice shared by a German woman who had witnessed the fall of the Berlin Wall. The gathering was closed by singing "Shalom to You."

Mission projects developed within the first weeks. After the third worship service, a young gay man living with AIDS asked the community to join him in feeding the homeless as a response to the communion service. In late August, a small group began teaching GED classes in the jail, and another group organized and funded a mission team to Guatemala.

The community met each Sunday evening in this space through the end of September. However, notification was made in August that the space would no longer be available to them. The second United Methodist congregation had become aware that several members of the Community of Hope were openly gay, and asked that the community find another place to meet.

LOCATING A HOME

It became apparent to the community that a space of their own was needed. A small building on North Yale Avenue was located that could be rented; it had one moderate size room that could accommodate, though crowded, a maximum of sixty people and two small rooms that could be used for other needs such as children's activities. On Sunday, October 3, 1993, the community gathered in the parking lot of the little building to consecrate this space through a service of song, dance, Scripture, prayer, breaking bread together and an infant baptism. A newsletter article described the evening in this way:

> We reflected together during the evening on the invitation that God extended to the Israelites—the invitation to become "home-makers" in the midst of a sometimes confusing, sometimes hostile, sometimes frightful and alienating place. "Build houses," the Lord said, "and plant gardens . . . raise families . . . and work for the welfare of the place where you live!" (Jer. 29:5-7). In other words, become "home-makers." And as we shared together our gratitude for the blessing of a place to house our Community, we found ourselves being reminded of two important things. . . . First, that in a world that is *still* sometimes confusing, sometimes hostile, sometimes frightful and alienating, "home-making" in the midst of homelessness is *still* the ministry to which God calls us. And second, that it is always in community and not a building where we will find "home."

Much of the development of the community grew out of some of the earliest visioning. The newly appointed pastor's first letter to people who expressed an interest in the community described the hope in this way: "It is my hope that Bible study will be at the very core of our life, and that each person will be significantly involved in healing our world in some hands-on, concrete way. I also trust that we will worship together (and that our worship will reflect our multicultural vision); that we will be in prayer with and for one another and our world; and that the sacraments will feed and empower our sense of community. But the how's, when's, where's and what else's are still to be decided by the community itself."

The community made a commitment to worship together on Sunday evenings. The sacrament of Holy Communion became so essential to the life and work that it began to be celebrated almost every Sunday. Communion was also offered during the week to strengthen people to endure the major struggles they faced. The healing power of the Eucharist was discovered as a way to ritualize the deep sharing of individual and corporate brokenness, a way to celebrate the powerful sense of healing that came in naming that brokenness honestly in the presence of each other, and as an offering to God. The bread of life and the cup of hope brought a powerful sense of relief and renewal in the announcement of forgiveness and acceptance. A member said, "Often there is hugging and laughter and tears as the grace of the bread, the wine, and the community wash over us and offer an Amen to our worship." Worship at COH, as described in a 1998 brochure, is experienced as relational and communal, designed to create an atmosphere of "honesty and acceptance where people can speak their fears, their hurts, their shame, their joys, their hopes aloud to God and one another, where we can bear one another's burdens and hold one another in prayer through our tragedies and embracing our differences; where people can bring all of who they are to worship God, to feast at God's table, and to hear themselves called 'beloved child of God.' "

From the earliest visioning by the bishop and associate pastor, the base communities of Central America had influenced the hope of what this newly created community might become. In the first letter sent by the pastor to people interested in the base community ministry being started in Tulsa, she explained the "base community is a third-world model of being the church that is centered around Bible study that empowers the poor and oppressed to be in ministry." As the new community began to interpret and adapt this model, the first description put in writing described the community as "a group of persons who gather together both because they desire to work for concrete social change, and because they hunger for a deeper spirituality than is available to them in most of their settings. The foundation or 'base' of a 'base community' is prayer, Scripture study, and working in concrete, specific ways for love and justice." An in-depth Bible study was begun using *Disciple* Bible study, a year-long, weekly two-hour class with reading assignments, that was designed to focus on the intersection of meaning between the Bible and people's lives.

As the character of the Community of Hope began to take shape, the pastor developed the following model:

EXILE

SOLIDARITY   SANCTUARY

DISCIPLESHIP   HOSPITALITY

COMPASSION

She explains the cyclic movement of the model:

> My early anticipations were that at whatever point one enters the journey, they may move through the cycle again and again. . . . For instance, if one comes into the Community of Hope from an experience of *exile* (which many are and will) they will most likely seek and need a time of *sanctuary* wherein they are simply offered acceptance and a safe place to rest and think and reflect and heal. As healing takes place, the sojourner will then move into a place of offering *hospitality* to others who are seeking *sanctuary*. In the "movement," they will encounter and wrestle with their prejudices, learn to value diversity, and begin to offer mutual respect to others. *Hospitality* would include acts of "hearing others into their own speech" and enabling growth by sharing power. The next move will be to reach out to others with increasing *compassion*, a deep "womb" sense of passion for their pain, and then to *discipleship*, a commitment to their companion that is grounded in the call to reconcile with "the other." The final move comes when they are genuinely reconciled to the other as brother or sister in Christ . . . and therefore, able to re-enter into *exile* as one who seeks to be in *solidarity* with the exiled. The journey then begins again as the sojourner returns for rest and *sanctuary*,

perhaps bringing one of the exiled with her or him into the *community*."

The very first suggestion for reaching out into service of the larger community was to commit to a regular time each month to provide a meal for persons living at the Shelter for the Homeless. This ministry had been suggested by the a young gay man living with AIDS. According to the pastor, "That first meal was cooked by two young women who suffer so severely from the effects of horrendous abuse that they rarely leave their home; the food was paid for by a young man bedridden with AIDS who donated his food stamps; and the meal was served for one hundred homeless men and women by a group of men and women living with AIDS." This was a significant undertaking for a small group of people who struggled every day with the emotional and physical effects of HIV/AIDS, addictions, and poverty, including meager meals with little to share. But the challenge was met and others were encouraged by what could be done with so little when it was done together.

Out of this beginning the community began to develop a variety of opportunities for hands-on involvement in mission and justice work. The first brochure published by the Community of Hope listed the following projects: Volunteers in Mission teams working locally and internationally; the Affirming Diversity focus group working for full human and civil rights of all persons and for full inclusion of all persons in the life and work of the Church; the RAIN Care Team, the "Angel Baskets," and Rainbow Village housing project supporting those living with HIV/AIDS; the Domestic Violence Intervention Service transitional living apartment serving victims of domestic violence; "community garden" to supplement food stamp budgets, and the Day Center for the Homeless.

A community decision was made in budgeting of resources and time that committed the same amount spent within the community to be spent outside the community. The community maintained its discipline of spending one dollar beyond its walls for every dollar spent within the community. It also sought to invest one hour of time (companions and staff) in the larger community for every hour spent within the Community of Hope.

THE ADVISORY COMMITTEE

In a July meeting with the bishop, the pastor described the isolation she felt in her ministry as she worked to provide pastoral leadership and to maintain her ties with the United Methodist connection. She needed personal support and administrative advice as she struggled to cope both with a congregation where someone was dying of AIDS on the average of twice a month and with a perceived growing resistance to Community of Hope from other congregations and many of her peers in ministry. She requested that an Advisory Committee be formed to give support and advice and to act as a liaison with the Annual Conference. The committee would also act as a sounding board for the many practical decisions being made regarding organizational structure, developing vision models, setting up records and financial development, proposing policy regarding hiring of some part-time staff, growth issues, connectional issues with the UMC, and integrity issues in ministry. A list of possible members was drawn up composed of laity and clergy (including members of the bishop's cabinet) from across the Oklahoma Conference; these persons were invited to serve in this capacity. The first meeting of the Advisory Committee was held in October 1993, at the building on North Yale.

The Advisory Committee met monthly, at first, and then quarterly. Representatives of the Community were present and participated in each meeting. The meetings began at 10 A.M. and ended around 3 P.M. usually including a short time of meditation, personal life stories shared by persons from the Community of Hope and Advisory Committee members, a meal, reports from the pastor, and discussion of issues related to the life of the community. At first, in consultation with the pastor, leadership was passed around to those who would agree to take charge of ordering the meeting. Later, a member of the committee emerged as the chair and conducted the agenda. The Advisory Committee continually found itself in dialogue with the scriptural meditation, the shared stories, and the critical issues with which the experimental community struggled. It was also caught up in the question of how the community was to maintain integrity in its relationship to the UMC and make a contribution to that connection as well.

The community understood itself to be in covenant relationship rather than in a "chartered" relationship as a "local church" with the UMC. For the most part, the community had a strong commitment to being denominationally related as a community of faith rather than nondenominational, because it valued connection to the horizontal and vertical dimensions of the Christian community. It worked diligently to honor the spirit of the United Methodist connection, and at the same time to embrace and live into the founding invitation to help the larger church explore new ways to live as the "new community of Christ."

With the encouragement of the Advisory Committee, the community communicated with the Oklahoma Conference in several ways. Among the booths featuring special projects at Annual Conference was a booth sponsored by the Community of Hope. It had pictures, a video presentation, brochures, and pins giving information about the ministry of the community. A number of community participants were present to host the booth. The pastor and several companions made a presentation as a part of the Conference agenda. At another Annual Conference meeting, delegates were invited to a breakfast held at the Community of Hope at which the story of its ministry was narrated. Invitations to join the community in its regular services of worship were extended to United Methodist congregations. The pastor sent letters to United Methodist clergy to let them know that New Hope, the music ministry, was available upon invitation to sing at other churches for fellowship dinners, worship, or other occasions.

In the spring of 1994, two members of the community started New Hope, a musical ensemble committed to finding, singing, and eventually writing music that expressed the journey of faith, hope, and the struggle for justice to which the community was committed. The music of this group became a voice for communicating the spirituality and mission of the community and reminding it of its purpose.

During this same time period, Community of Hope made the decision to become a Reconciling Congregation. The pastor had been aware of the Reconciling Congregation Program from its inception. She shared stories of the movement at meetings and in worship. For the most part, participants in COH regarded the mission of the Reconciling Congregation Program as coinciding with their own. When the pastor recommended that COH make an official commitment to the Reconciling Congregation Program (RCP), there was general positive support. However, the issue that the community began to acknowledge in its discussions was the importance of being related to the larger church. As one member said, "The issue we had to face was not the one about what it means to be the church but about what it means to be a part of the larger church." Discussions revealed a consensus that it was important to continue to maintain an institutional connection and to relate to the UMC at this level in this way. The most difficult part of the decision was allocating the $250 required for Conference membership each year; prioritizing their meager resources always required careful discernment about what was most essential to their mission.

After publishing some informative articles in the newsletter and making announcements in worship, the community voted to become a Reconciling Congregation. Ironically, when the pastor called the director of RCP to tell him of the positive vote, he questioned whether the community was eligible to join since membership required being a chartered church of the UMC, which COH was not. A few weeks later, in May 1994, the community was notified of acceptance of its membership in the RCP. A relationship of solidarity with this movement grew as the community sent four representatives to the RCP national meetings in Atlanta and found informative support through issues of the RCP newsletter, "Open Hands." The pastor says, "We found the newsletter to be especially helpful after the addition to the 'Discipline' forbidding Holy Unions, just to know the position of other committed Methodists on the larger scene."

At the end of the first year, an average of forty-five were meeting for worship and there was beginning discussion of moving into a larger space. The community took financial responsibility for increasing the pastor's salary to the minimum level required for "full time" status in the UMC. One of the active participants began volunteering twenty hours a week doing administration and music leadership. During the first year the community was significantly involved with the homeless, with the incarcerated, with persons dealing with HIV/AIDS, with Domestic Violence Intervention Service, with Project Get Together, and with the Human Rights Commission's efforts toward civil rights for gay and lesbian persons. The community sent a Volunteer in Mission team to Guatemala, and were preparing a second team to go to Nicaragua, hosted a game night for neighborhood children, started a support group for women with HIV, hosted a multiracial dialogue on racism, and helped initiate an outreach ministry to gay and lesbian youth in Tulsa.

During the second year of ministry, the focus shifted from starting new things to supporting people in ministries already undertaken. In an effort to empower and support growth toward whole and healthy living, an ongoing series of spiritual nurture and life-skill study groups were developed. The community sponsored a number of groups on understanding Scripture, dealing with addiction, nurturing spirituality and prayer, parenting skills, healthy relationships, co-dependency, and grief management. The volunteer was hired as part-time office manager and began to be intentional about seeking financial support and resources. A number of grants were applied for and received for the work with HIV/AIDS and racism. Support was sought from persons in the larger community. A network of connections with other organizations was expanded as participants in the community took leadership positions in RAIN (Regional AIDS Interfaith Network), the AIDS Coalition, Shanti, Rainbow Village, the HIV Resource Consortium, the UM AIDS Task Force, DVIS

(Domestic Violence Intervention Services), TMM (Tulsa Metropolitan Ministry), Tulsa Community AIDS Partnership, and the Human Rights Commission. The pastor was invited to become an adjunct faculty member at Phillips Theological Seminary. This fostered a relationship between COH and the seminary as the community became a site for student field education.

The community celebrated its joy together with fellowship events such as shared meals, birthday celebrations, a weekly evening of dancing, picnics, and movie nights. These times were reinforced with images from worship of "the great thanksgiving," "invitation to the banquet," current scholarship about the historical Jesus, images of earthiness and a zest for life.

From the beginning, the community struggled with the question of what it means to be God's church. Identification as a "base community" rather than as a "church" forced them to wrestle with what each term meant, with whom to affiliate, and what the community was called to become. Many participants came from having been rejected by churches because of sexual orientation or AIDS; others came with layers of internalized shame and self-hatred learned in churches and/or in "religious" families. The kinds and levels of woundedness that people brought with them into the Community of Hope led them toward two very different expressions of their search for healing: (1) a deep longing to be accepted by and participate in the same church that had rejected them; and (2) an intense rejection of anything that at all resembled the church that had rejected them. Negotiating the two needs took intentional dialogue, care, education, and flexibility as worship styles, faith language, symbols, and participation methods developed.

The pastor helped people negotiate their conflicted feelings through her sermons:

> Jesus invested his life in teaching about and calling others to participate in God's vision for all creation—a "new community" where human beings live together as "neighbors" seeking wholeness and abundant life (salvation) for each person and

all creation. As those who are trying to be faithful to God by imitating the way of Jesus, we are committed to live and act as that "new community." We hope and struggle, therefore, to be a community where diversity is affirmed and celebrated, where truth-telling liberates people from the shame of secrets; where each of us and all of us are engaged in seeking and building relationships of justice, mutuality, and compassion with our neighbors toward the reconciliation and healing (salvation) of God's creation. We believe this is the only way to live out Jesus' commandment to "love God and neighbor."

As a way to bear witness to God's call to live as neighbors, we have chosen to be a "Reconciling" Community—welcoming of all persons including gay, lesbian, bisexual and transgendered persons—and a shalom community—committed to ministries of healing, support and empowerment, to and with persons and families who are challenged by HIV/AIDS, addiction, and the effects of spiritual, physical, and emotional violence and abuse. Believing that all of us are broken in different ways and all of us are gifted in different ways, we seek to be "wounded healers" both by being a "safe place" for one another's healing and growth, and by participation in healing the world through hands-on care, education, and political change.

The pastor preached regularly from the lectionary and related the Scripture to the life issues of the community and personal pain of its members. She knew about their life issues because she spent time with people in their daily environment, in their places of work, or homelessness, or sickness or incarceration. She was present to their daily struggles with physical pain, addiction, incarceration, and dysfunction. She developed a deep empathy for hurting people. Her activity intensified the accepted image of a pastoral call. Her actions revealed her commitment to be with people in the midst of their lives and to continually discern what the biblical image of "right relationship" would mean in daily life. An experience that graphically illustrates this occurred when she and her husband sat in a hospital room with a member dying of AIDS and his companion. During the last moments of his life when nothing else could be done, she abandoned traditional pastoral reticence and cradled him in her arms during his last breaths. She described this compassion as "a deep 'womb' sense of passion for [his] pain."

A participant in Community of Hope described the pastoral leadership as charismatic: "Her charisma developed with members of the community because they perceived her acute sensitivity to the brokenness of other people and a willingness to participate in their healing." This was lived out through her personal presence and energy, being attuned enough to critical issues to relate Scripture to life crises, providing safe space for truth telling, naming the hurt and making worship a time for sharing it. She continually connected worship with the work place and life issues of participants.

Given the conflict within the UMC about homosexuality, Community of Hope decided that they would not celebrate holy unions or weddings for one year. But, in January 1994, the pastor and bishop began to create a ceremony in which the Community of Hope would witness the vows of gay couples. The first holy union was held on July 9, 1994, for two gay men who were living with AIDS and had been a part of the founding group. Members of the community and of the Advisory Committee (including several United Methodist clergy) were present for the Holy Union, as well as the memorial celebration for one of the couple who died the following May. Out of these services, experiences of pastoral counseling, Bible study groups, the developing life of the community, and discussions within the Advisory Committee, work began to create a theology and ethics to undergird their practices of faith (see appendix 6 for "The Ritual of 'Joining-Together' " from "Toward a Theology of 'Joined-Together' ").

LIFE-SUSTAINING SYMBOLS

In the early days of its life together, several symbols began to emerge for the Community of Hope. The broken-yet-made-whole chalice given to the community in their very first service became the chalice placed on the altar table with the bread and used during communion. Its power for the community in their rituals made it the obvious symbol for a community logo. Later, when a committee was asked to create a brochure about the community for public distribute, this symbol was chosen for the cover with the following explanation:

> The broken-yet-made-whole chalice is the symbol adopted by our community. It represents that we are all broken and wounded people, yet each of us have strengths and skills and gifts and knowledge, sometimes beyond our own awareness. It is in community, as the love and grace of God work in and through us, that we are empowered to claim both our brokenness and our giftedness, so that together we can be and do more than any one of us can be or do alone!

Another person brought a candle with a rainbow on it. The candle was translucent and radiated light from within. Later someone made candles like it, adding a carved "Shalom." This became the Christ candle, representing the unity in diversity of the risen Christ. Both the Christ candle and the broken-yet-made-whole, chalice were early key symbols of the community.

When the community moved to the first rented space on North Yale Avenue, a table was needed for communion. Working with a frugal budget, a table was found at a nearby antique/junk store. It was a small table that had eight sides, open at the bottom and supported by spokes. It was almost round. It was presented to the community described as having no corners, almost, but not quite, round—"not there yet." The not-quite-round-table came to symbolize the goal of being a place of welcome to all people and the confession that this hope is not always realized.

A decision was made to place a drawing of the Living Jesus (a black interpretation) on the wall above the table instead of hanging a cross there. This decision came out of a need to express the living presence of Jesus in the midst of the community. A picture of the Great Spirit was placed on another wall making visible multicultural images of God. After a mission trip to Nicaragua, a cross on which faces of persons from that country had been carved was added to the communion table.

A community banner was made. The banner depicted a circle of multicolored people holding hands around the broken-yet-made-whole, chalice with a red ribbon and the word, "Shalom." This was hung on the wall and then carried out to be used at wider community gatherings, parades, and marches.

As the community grieved the deaths of participants living with AIDS, a ritual of remembering was created and included in the Sunday evening worship service and a "remembering wall" was constructed on which hand-painted tiles naming each companion who died of HIV/AIDS were placed. Later, a "companioning wall" of hand prints in various colors developed as a part of the ritual of companionship. The community did not create official membership or accept letters of transfer but invited anyone who wanted to participate to add their hand print to the wall. This wall and ritual came to symbolize the embodied presence of Christ experienced in one another and the commitment to hands-on participation in the journey of struggle and hope.

Much later, having entered into a new visioning process, the community agreed to bring scraps of cloth from clothing or other fabric objects that were a part of significant life happenings. These were braided into a rug to represent the ongoing process of weaving a vision for life together out of our understandings of who God is, who we are, what values we hold central.

With increased participation, the facilities on North Yale became too cramped to support the work of the community. In August of 1995, the third location was found—a dilapidated warehouse in an "at risk" neighborhood on North Utica. All the work to refurbish the building was done by participants in the community over several months. Thousands of hours and dollars were donated to rebuild, carpet, paint, equip, and furnish the building to a simple but adequate standard.

Within six months in the new location on North Utica, attendance had increased to an average of seventy, and support groups and other ministries were expanded. In January of 1996 a newly formed Unitarian Universalist congregation began to rent space on Sunday morning and an independent Catholic congregation rented space on Saturday evening. Late in 1996 a duplex was donated to Community of Hope, which was restored with volunteer labor, commissioned as "Hope House," and managed as low cost housing for two families living with HIV/AIDS. By the end of 1997 the average attendance was eighty-five to ninety, and in addition to the ongoing mission and ministry groups, a youth group sponsored by Youth Services of Tulsa was hosted, along with a Native American men's support group, several 12-step support groups, and occasional community service meetings.

After one year in the warehouse they made home, the property owner expressed a need to sell the property and an investigation into zoning and occupancy requirements ruled out purchasing by the community. So the search for a "home" began for the fourth time. This took eighteen months of working with several realtors and losing several properties before finally locating an adequate and affordable property.

DISPLACEMENT AND DECISION

At the General Conference of April 1996, a statement was added to the *Book of Discipline* declaring that "ceremonies that celebrate homosexual unions shall not be conducted by our ministers or in our churches." During the remainder of that year and all of 1997, much of the time and energy of the community was invested in wrestling with a response to that ruling. Several community meetings were held to hear one another's rage and fear over "having to choose between our relationships and our membership in the UMC." In addition, the bishop who had supported the founding of the community was moved to another jurisdiction and a new bishop was assigned to the Oklahoma Conference. The uncertainty of how the bishop would relate to the community posed another dimension of concern. How would the new bishop's interpretation and implementation of the addition to the *Discipline* affect the Community of Hope?

A theology and ethics of "joining together" was created by a small task force composed of the pastor, a founding member of the community, and two seminary professors (a New Testament scholar and a theologian) who participated in the community. The initial drafts of these statements were presented in study groups to the community. The drafts were reworked by the committee, presented to the community, and studied and discussed over a period of time. When the community reached consensus, their theology was shared with the bishop and the cabinet. On the basis of the theology and ethics of "Joining Together" (see appendix 6) a decision was made to continue celebrating all life commitments, gay and straight. A new factor soon became a foreboding reality. Charges could be filed against the pastor that could result in her ordination being revoked.

Holy unions for both heterosexual and homosexual couples continued to be celebrated by the community. The pastor was in open communication with the bishop's cabinet about these actions. All couples were required to participate in premarital counseling and the whole congregation continued to work hard to respect the stated policy of the denomination without sacrificing its own integrity.

The Advisory Committee continued to be informed. Letters describing the work of COH and requesting continued communication with and support for the experimental community were sent by Advisory Committee members to the bishop and the cabinet. There was little direct communication from the bishop, but two district superintendents who were members of the Advisory Committee continued to offer support and counsel and to attend all Advisory Committee meetings. At the time for annual reports to the Conference, the pastor received from the bishop a form asking her to report on her "extension ministry" and to include a written evaluation from a supervisor other than her district superintendent. In the past she had been asked for a pastor's report to the Conference. What did "extension ministry" mean? Who would write her evaluation other than the congregation of persons she pastored? What was the bishop thinking about the United Methodist Community of Hope Shalom Base

Community and their pastor? It was apparent that the Community of Hope would not receive the personal support from the bishop's office that it had been afforded in the past.

In March 1998, the community purchased a very worn Assembly of God building and moved to its fourth location—an abandoned, slightly vandalized building with a leaking roof, no functioning heat and air units, and a host of other problems. Because of the tentativeness of the relationship with the UMC, the Advisory Committee recommended that the words United Methodist be legally removed from the corporate name before purchasing the building. In addition to raising $30,000 for down payment and closing costs, within the first three months, an additional $15,000 had to be raised for repairs. This required a tremendous amount of volunteer time for cleaning, roofing, and repairing the building. The neighborhood around the building had some difficulty with the presence of the Community of Hope; there were a few incidents of verbal insults and harassment. However, as the property was improved and the community proved itself to be a good neighbor, the harassment stopped.

At the same time the pastor's father became terminally ill; in the wake of the cumulative effect of the long-term and immediate stresses, her need for self-care became acute. In addition to her daily discipline of morning prayer and study, it was her practice to take time apart on a regular basis for a day of silence, personal prayer retreat, continuing education and study, as well as for play and recreation. But more concentrated periods of time were needed. As was their practice, this need was shared in worship with the community. Others, both inside and outside COH, were called on to take responsibility for worship services, for preaching, for conducting meetings, and for pastoral care to provide the needed release.

These events took a heavy toll on the life, energy, and morale of the community. It was soon evident that factions were developing. The pastor proposed bringing in a consultant to help them make new decisions about their life together and their future. The consultant led the community in a series of Visioning Workshops over a weekend retreat held in the COH facilities. These were followed by several meetings of committees generated by the workshops to shape objectives and plans for the future. The community met several times in the following weeks to reach consensus on the work of these committees and to create a corporate visioning statement.

Increasing administrative demands brought on by the growth of the community and complicated by the move and immediate needs of the building had pushed the community to design an administrative structure to facilitate the involvement of more people in leadership. By June, 1998, there was a Coordinating Council, with an expectation that the capacity of the Council to hear and respond to the needs of the community and the call of the gospel would be augmented by one group to support ministry teams and another to facilitate communication.

In February 1999, an official complaint was filed against the pastor for signing as an officiant "in absentia" of a holy union. On March 3, 1999, press coverage resulted in a holy union conducted by the pastor at the Community of Hope being aired on a television news program. Rather than expend any further energy and money on a church trial, the pastor made a decision to withdraw from The United Methodist Church and applied to transfer her orders to the United Church of Christ.

At that point the pastor's ordination was the only connection the Community of Hope had to The United Methodist Church, so they began a process of exploration and discernment regarding denominational affiliation. The Advisory Board agreed to act as the coordinating committee for the transitional process. In 2001, after eight years as a quasi-official congregation of The United Methodist Church, the Community of Hope officially affiliated with the United Church of Christ.

In 2001 the Community of Hope had a "companionship" of about two-hundred people who participated and associated in a variety of ways. The worship attendance was an average of seventy people. The makeup of the congregation continued to be socially, religiously and economically diverse; 40 percent heterosexual, 60 percent homosexual; 25 percent were on subsidized income; 10 percent were moderately wealthy, and the majority had moderate financial means. Participants included some home-

less and mentally ill people, doctors, therapists, seminary professors, and lawyers, some incarcerated and post-incarcerated people; priests and pastors from eight denominations, youth, single
parents, families with and without children, and a growing
twenty-something group. About 30 percent of the group was in
recovery or struggling for recovery from chemical addictions; and
20 percent were HIV- infected, men, women, and children. Over
fifty participants died of AIDS in the eight years that the community was a part of the UMC.

It is Sunday evening and the pastor is preaching.

> Our commitment to this wilderness-wandering toward a new
> way of being God's Church brings with it a subtle but constant
> sense of "homelessness." More often than not, there are no
> road maps, no beaten paths, and no star to follow. In addition,
> we live and work constantly aware of an unidentified and fluid
> resistance to who we are perceived to be, that can drain and/or
> divert our energy. We are more aware than ever that choosing
> to companion with the Community of Hope requires a signifi-
> cant level of investment, a commitment to the long haul, and
> a willingness to risk. . . . We are also aware that our greatest
> threats are weariness of the struggle and the temptation to
> return to known, comfortable models of the past. Therefore, as
> we wander and wander together, we find it necessary to remind
> ourselves of three things. First, that it is the journey not the des-
> tination to which we are called; second, that God's people have
> always discovered their salvation (healing and wholeness) as
> they companioned one another on the way; and finally, that
> "in life, in death, in life beyond death, we are not alone."

The congregation sings.

> Where the hurt can find a shelter
> Where the broken is restored
> Where we all can be encouraged
> Where there is faith and hope and love.
> Where there's room to grow together
> By the Spirit we will know
> We are all part of God's family.

CHAPTER SEVEN

CONGREGATIONS STRUGGLING WITH HOPE: EMBODIED KNOWING

The congregations of this book were courageous in many ways, but nothing is more obvious than their willingness to wrestle with difficult issues. Representing diverse regions, congregational sizes, and ethnic communities, all have struggled with questions of ministry with gay, lesbian, bisexual, and transgendered persons. Four of these congregations voted to become Reconciling Congregations and one chose not to take formal action. Following decisions made at the 2000 General Conference of The United Methodist Church, none of the congregations can officially call themselves Reconciling Congregations, but all actively practice reconciliation.

The following questions are addressed in this chapter:

1) What experiences and concerns move a congregation to consider a risky ethical stand?
2) What kind of teaching and learning allow a congregation to reach such a decision, and then, to live into it?
3) What helps and hinders a community's ability to make meaning and build community in the midst of confronting difficult issues?
4) What theological and ethical commitments are informing these congregations?

As to the first question, the congregations all had experiences of personal story-telling, sharing pain, and confronting dissonance; some had long-standing precedents for embracing ethnic and class diversity, practicing ministries of hospitality, and taking risky ethical stands on social issues. As to the second question, close analysis reveals the importance of learning in community, represented in these congregations by extensive dialogue and willingness to deal with complexities and competing points of view. All of the congregations functioned with some kind of holding center with permeable boundaries, thus permitting flexibility, diversity, and disagreement.

On the third question, the congregational studies reveal the power of symbolic forms in these five congregations—symbolic events, people, spaces, and language. This is particularly true for those that made the reconciling decision. Other influential factors seemed to be ministries of hospitality and openness to vulnerability by clergy and lay leaders. Finally, with regard to the fourth question, analysis reveals several theological themes. Among them are trusting in God's grace, theological reflection in response to pressing human concerns, and commitments to community solidarity, despite theological and ethical differences.

Other insights will emerge in the analysis, but this summary reveals something of the embodied tradition within these particular communities. The value is intensified when one considers that these five congregations represent one small portion of The

United Methodist Church, which as a whole is highly conflicted on questions of homosexuality. The decisions of these congregations may be less important to the larger church than the insights regarding how some Wesleyan Christian communities have engaged controversial issues. In this chapter, attention will be given to details of the congregational narratives, making no claims for their normativeness, but rather making claims for the richness one can discover in the internal life of Christian congregations, especially as they are studied in probing detail.

EXPERIENCES OF PAIN: MINISTRIES OF HOSPITALITY

Certainly no congregation can claim to be pain-free, but the congregations of this study have histories of pain and vulnerability that have emboldened them and intensified their concern for people within and beyond their congregations. Community of Hope was actually founded to respond to people who were hurting in the Tulsa area. Epworth UMC was declared a "dying church," but the people were determined not to die. Epworth's active reflection on the possibility of becoming a Reconciling Congregation originated in their experience of a seminary intern who was struggling with his sexuality. Their discussions did not begin as an abstract "issue," but as a pastoral concern rooted in the community itself.

Likewise, Claremont UMC traces its initial deliberations to a Parents, Families and Friends of Lesbians and Gays (PFLAG) group, made up of people in the church and community who were struggling with relationships in their own families and friendship circles. North's closure of continued conversation eight months into their preparation for making a decision limited further exploration of the explicit and visible pain within the congregation. In one session people were able to share their stories about sexual differences in straightforward and earnest ways but the process was prematurely terminated. In sum, these are all congregations that have known pain, and pain of many kinds. They are also congregations where people are willing to share their stories with one another and to respond to painful stories with ministries of hospitality.

The Community of Hope in Tulsa was born from an early iden-tification with people on the fringes of society (people suffering with HIV/AIDS) and a painful split in the large congregation that was ministering with these people. The split came when a gay couple was baptized and negative reactions began to escalate. The result was much deliberation within and beyond the local church, and the eventual decision by the bishop and cabinet to support the formation of a new ministry in the Tulsa Shalom Base Community. The focus of this community's ministry would be the embodiment of Micah 6:8: "What does the LORD require of you but to do justice, and to love kindness, and to walk humbly with your God?"

The suffering of people with HIV/AIDS that originally inspired members of the large United Methodist congregation to serve people on the fringes eventually led to painful controversy and division. It led in time to the formation of a distinctive community patterned after Latin American Base Communities, which sought to embody hospitality within and beyond the con-gregation, and to take a stand against racism, sexism, classism, and homophobia. Nowhere is the link between pain and min-istries of hospitality more striking than in Community of Hope's ministry with homeless people in their community. Two young women, who were severely abused and nearly homebound, pre-pared the congregation's first meal for the homeless shelter; a young man bedridden with AIDS donated his food stamps to pay for the food.

Epworth is another example of hospitality born of pain. When a group of United Methodist Women arrived at their church one morning to work on one of their projects, they were jolted by the news that a man had frozen to death in the dumpster behind their church. We are told in chapter 5 that the women "went back to the church, determined that if they could help it, people were not going to freeze to death while the church gymnasium was empty." This event led to a series of actions and reactions that culminated in the congregation's decision to open their gymnasium to homeless people. They are still known as one of the safest homeless shelters in Chicago.

Similarly, the PFLAG group at Claremont UMC was started by parents and friends who needed a community with whom to share their questions about homosexuality, especially their struggle to accept and respond lovingly to their gay and lesbian sons and daughters, brothers and sisters. Members of the original PFLAG group eventually reached out to families who were struggling silently; they also invited gay and lesbian members into the membership of the church. The presence of these new members, plus the encouragement of the PFLAG group, finally led the entire congregation into the process of becoming a Reconciling Congregation.

The Saratoga Springs congregation had a distinctive experience of pain when their pastor, Jim Borden, was murdered. The link between that dreadful experience and present stances of the congregation may or may not be causal, but the link is in people's minds. The current pastor says that people "still deal with it . . . his memory's still there." Certainly, Jane Borden, the wife and ministerial colleague of Jim, was a leader in articulating social ministry at Saratoga Springs, including her attention to inclusive language and then, to sexual orientation. In chapter 2, we discover that "the 'struggle' over language laid the foundations for later studies of homosexuality." In short, the violent death of a beloved pastor seems to have awakened a strong feeling of compassion in the congregation. Their compassion has found expression in a variety of forms with a focus on a variety of issues, each one contributing to those that follow.

These stories are only some of the moments of pain in our five congregations. What is inescapable in these stories, however, is not the pain itself, but the ways in which the experiences of pain contributed to awakening, to more active storytelling and sharing of personal pain, to increased vulnerability and courage (such as the request to form a new ministry in Tulsa), and to increased passion for ministries of hospitality. The Saratoga Springs church has become more ethnically diverse since becoming a Reconciling Congregation. The current pastor of Claremont

UMC says that the newest members of the congregation have come to the church because of its welcoming spirit. This is true for gay and straight members. He tells of a couple with children who sought out a Reconciling Congregation when they moved into the area because they did not find the hospitality of their former Reconciling Congregation in other congregations. They now drive an hour each way to church in order to participate in a Reconciling Congregation.

The experiences of the congregations in our study suggest that pain has the potential to stir the passions of people and to motivate ministries of hospitality. Congregations that have experienced pain, and have identified with people in pain, often become increasingly open to encountering pain in other areas of life. The Claremont congregation's experience as a Sanctuary Church, responding to the pain of refugees, contributed to its ability to face another kind of pain and to respond to people who were gay, lesbian, bisexual, and transgendered. During their months of deliberation, people made the connection between the two kinds of outreach.

The Community of Hope in Tulsa discovered that, over time, they were responding to larger and increasingly diverse circles of pain. They came to understand their vocation as "homemaking in the midst of homelessness." Their experiences have so impassioned them that they concluded they could no longer be a part of The United Methodist Church with its present condemnations and limitations of gay, lesbian, bisexual, and transgendered people. In short, the tradition that inspired their openness to pain and ministries of hospitality has now seemingly become a counterwitness to the vocation to which they are called.

In conclusion, pain contributes to passion, and passion to ministries of hospitality. It is possible that other congregations would have a very different orientation (in general) if they saw their mission in terms of encountering pain, telling their stories and hearing the stories of others, and translating those experiences into embodied acts of hospitality, within and beyond their own congregation. These seem to be critical practices of communities able to bring hope into hopeless situations.

LEARNING IN COMMUNITY

These practices of encountering pain, telling stories, and offering hospitality suggest an approach to teaching and learning that is communal. Church leaders, then, have a responsibility to create space where people can explore differences and alternatives through dialogue. Consider the story of Jacob, who wrestled with the angel; he first tended to his family and other responsibilities, then he cleared a space for waiting (Genesis 32:22-33). This kind of space-clearing and anticipating are important to the leader's role, as well as persistent efforts in creating and nurturing a community life that is trusting, compassionate, honest, and open for the deepest possible learning.

The value of such learning is why the World Council of Churches has put such stress on "learning in community" in recent decades. It is why people in many different fields accent the influence of "communities of practice." In fact, learning in community has been heralded throughout the history of Christian communities. For example, communal gatherings— societies, classes, and bands—were critically important in the early Methodist movement. In those gatherings, prayer, singing, and study were all important. In the societies, that had a more instructional quality, exhortation was also a major part of the gatherings; these included biblical interpretation and ethical guidance. In the classes and bands, groups studied Scripture together and responded each week to questions in the presence of one another. These were not easy questions; they often invoked pain and led to deep deliberation, prayer, and advising of one another. The first questions were: "Have you the forgiveness of your sins? Have you peace with God through our Lord Jesus Christ? Have you the witness of God's Spirit with your spirit that you are a child of God? Is the love of God shed abroad in your heart?"

Though these questions focused on individuals, they took place within communities, and both individuals and communities were transformed in the process. The groups and questions were grounded in John Wesley's belief that Christian life is social:

"The Gospel of Christ knows no religion, but social; no holiness but social holiness. I mean that it cannot subsist at all without society, without living and conversing with others." In Methodist Church traditions, these early practices grew into an extensive ecology of educational approaches, forming communities with diverse peoples, teachers and purposes, and fostering a communal approach to teaching and learning.

Our study suggests that the practice of learning in community is influenced by historical, ecumenical, and denominational traditions, whether or not the five congregations were self-conscious about this. The Wesleyan tradition—the historical legacy and denominational home of the congregations in our study—is visible in the ways that teaching and learning were taking place. The congregations all embodied John Wesley's admonition toward "living and conversing with others." The congregations that became reconciling did so through months of living and conversation and through a longer process of dialogue about differences. The congregation where continued educational processes were forbidden, even though the formal action of the Administrative Board was to continue, was influenced by the pastor's concern that the larger congregational relationships might be impaired. Certainly, all of the congregations practiced communal learning, and did so actively. The learning was simultaneously individual and corporate; people were transformed, as were their congregations.

Building Interpersonal Relationships

Spontaneously and intentionally, many significant interpersonal relationships emerged in the congregations that were considering the reconciling decision. This was particularly true of those that decided to become reconciling, for their approaches opened the possibility for much honesty (sometimes disturbing honesty) and relationship building that pushed the boundaries of their existing relationships. North UMC, the largest of the congregations, took a more ordered and formal approach, ending the process before communication reached high intensity in the larger community.

In the dynamics of congregational wrestling, some people's lives changed dramatically (in all five congregations), but always through relationships with others. Internal wrestling was fueled by human encounters that deepened people's understandings and evoked passions and questions.

Most people were conscious of shifting relationships within their congregations as well. Some people felt that changes were coming too fast, and others were frustrated that they were not fast enough. Some felt isolated because their points of view were different from others. Some who decided to leave their congregations felt they were "losing my family." Some of the gay and lesbian people were deeply hurt by negative things that people said about homosexual persons during the deliberations, and some were overwhelmed by the positive decisions of their congregation. Some heterosexual parents had to deal with their own relations with a gay, lesbian, bisexual, or transgendered son or daughter, during the same period when they were overhearing or participating in their church's deliberations.

As individuals in our study described their change process—changes in value, beliefs, and practices—their stories revealed some common experiences and influences on transformation. All of these experiences emerged from interpersonal relationships:

- **Identifying with someone whose sexual orientation is different from one's own**—sometimes in the form of admiring or feeling drawn to that person. This might take the form of wanting to know about that person's experience.
- **Experiencing the pain of people different from one-self**—feeling the anguish of a family member, close friend, or close associate, who lives with social ostracism or oppression due to sexual orientation.
- **Experiencing intimate love in one's own life**—experiencing a love relationship that leads one to hope that others, gay and straight, will know such love in their lives.

- **Choosing to identify over time with people who are rejected or oppressed**—developing a sense that you are a person who cares for others, or that you live in a community that reaches out to people who have been marginalized.
- **Experiencing the reality of vicious hatred**—having a personal encounter with cruel words, physical violence, suicide or attempted suicide, murder or attempted murder, self-destructive denial of homosexual impulses, or destructive double-lives (as in an open straight life and a hidden gay life).

This list is striking because the experiences are quite personal, stirring a sense of tragedy and beauty, a longing for life that is free to flourish, and a hope for loving and authentic relationships for oneself and others. Such experiences are nourished in learning communities, especially in developing honest and caring interpersonal relationships. A learning community is one in which people gather to learn from and with one another—a community that is a seedbed for the kind of personal change and new sensitivities that our interviewees described. The communities in our studies did, in fact, tend to relationship building in many direct and indirect ways. More than anything, they created an ethos of honesty and compassion in the process of their decision making. The result was the development of learning communities, both planned and unplanned.

Building a Learning Community

The congregations of our study do not fit a single pattern, but they were all intentionally communal in approaching a challenging ethical decision through dialogue and honest exchange. The congregational studies shone a light on their internal workings, revealing much about their lives. When that process was terminated at North, it was the nature of the decision making that caused pain to many as well as questions about the honesty of that process. But all five congregations were involved in learning by active engagement with one another. In some cases, the dialogue began with an event that threw the congregation into turmoil, and thus turned them toward one another. In others, communal learning opportunities began small and grew. In still others, the process was intentionally planned with modifications and additions along the way. Most of the congregations were motivated toward communal learning by many factors.

Learning from unexpected, tragic events. Many years before the reconciling decision, Claremont UMC lost its sanctuary to an arsonist's fire. One church member received word of the fire and called others; soon, many members were gathered on the church grounds, crying as their nearly new building burned to cinders. They moved to their new "Round Building" until they could rebuild. During the months that followed, they did everything thing "in the round"—church school classes, fellowship groups, church suppers, prayer and study groups, and recreation. Motivated by the necessity, held by the shape of their architecture, and bound by their common loss, the community strengthened during these many months—a time described with fond memory by old-timers. When it came time to rebuild, they made a decision to build a small sanctuary, which could later be converted to a chapel and joined by a larger building, in place of the expansive grandiosity of their earlier plan. The church would, then, commit itself to more generous giving beyond itself.

Learning in community step-by-step. In the 1980s Claremont also engaged in a major effort of learning in community regarding the possibility of becoming a Sanctuary Church, receiving refugees from Latin America. Very intentional planning was done, and the plans grew as word spread and new ideas were suggested. The outcome was many months in which the community as a whole studied, prayed, and pondered decisions. Some of this was done in the Administrative Council, commissions and task forces; it was also done in adult forums and youth sessions. In all of this, the youth were engaged and encouraged to share their diverse views. They learned to show amazing respect for one another in their differences, recognizing also that their families had diverse views as well.

Intentionally planned learning in community. By the time Claremont began explorations of the reconciling decision, they had already experienced learning in community with its attendant pains, struggles, and joys. That may be one of the reasons they resolved to seek consensus, or something close to it. The desire expressed by members at the time, and by people interviewed in this study, was to dialogue with each other as much as possible in order to reach consensus or the highest possible agreement. This led to a longer and multifaceted process, but one that most members agreed with. Some did not agree with the final decision and a few left the congregation. This fact still stirs sadness for people, even a decade after the decision was made. People still express concern about those who left or drifted away from the congregation after the reconciling vote, a concern also voiced at Saratoga Springs. One gay man said the saddest aspect of the vote for him was losing these people. He had been personally active in reaching out to one of the couples, hoping they might return.

In this review of events, we see a pattern of learning in community, which has characterized the style of the congregation, especially in dealing with different views about decision making. We see also concern for the wholeness of the community, and a sense that everyone in the community is valuable and everyone has responsibility toward others. Such a pattern is found in the other congregations as well. For example, Community of Hope found that intentional learning communities were essential in negotiating the people's deep longing to be a valued and contributing part of the church and, at the same time, to reject church practices that had hurt them in the past.

Viewed as a group, the five congregations of our study exhibit qualities that contribute to change in individuals, their congregations, and their larger institutions. Dialogue was prominent in each congregation, including direct engagement with theological diversity. The congregations largely functioned around central shared commitments, but with permeable boundaries permitting flexibility and disagreement. Disagreement was handled in ways that were uniquely fitting to the particular congregation, such as the way in which the Epworth congregation handled the second reconciling vote. The Filipino members, who were largely uneasy about the decision, chose not to attend the meeting where the vote would be held. In this way, they could avoid blocking the decision without actually voting against their own consciences. They could thus foster the central commitments of the congregation to inclusive hospitality while disagreeing with the particular decision. Other members of the community interpreted their action as an act of generosity; only a community deeply engaged in dialogue and wrestling with differences could stir such generosity.

SYMBOLS AND MEANING-MAKING

Symbolic objects, events, people, places, and language were particularly influential in congregations that became Reconciling Congregations. Symbols were a major factor in expressing the central commitments of each congregation. Consider the rainbow candle of the Community of Hope, lighted each Sunday morning. Consider the cross outside the window at Saratoga Springs interpreted as a symbol that the congregation does not keep its faith within the walls. Consider the rainbow flag added to the sign of the Epworth Church, signifying diversity in covenant relationship.

Symbolic Objects

Every congregation is filled with symbolic objects, but we discovered the mighty power of symbols in the congregations of our study. Their symbols served many functions; forming identity, engaging people in an interactive discourse, stirring transformation, and reflecting shifts in the congregations. To these we now turn.

Identity-forming symbols. In some congregations, the visual symbols become central to the identity of the congregation. This is true for the Saratoga Springs congregation whose cross outside the window is a symbol to inspire people in Sunday worship, to show visitors, and to display on the bulletin cover. Standing outside the window and behind the chancel, the cross draws people's attention. Such a symbol has captivated the eyes and imaginations of the congregation. Members quickly share this symbol with newcomers. They readily reflect on it as well, as typified by Harold Smith, "We don't keep our faith in these walls. We take it outwards." A large window behind the chancel of Claremont Church functions in a similar way.

Interactive, multivalent symbols. In some ways, all symbols are interactive and multivalent; however, one symbol was particularly alive in the congregations we studied—the Bible, which functioned as an inspiring, challenging, and interactive symbol. All of the congregations were doing ministry in unusual, and sometimes risky and controversial, ways. At the same time, Bible study is often central to congregational life, and is often a primary influence on some of the riskier congregational practices. Continuing the observation at Saratoga Springs, Bible study was one of the primary ways that the congregation wrestled with their questions about homosexuality. This was done in sermons, in study within the RCP Task Force, in multiple studies within the congregation, and in at least one men's retreat. Other congregations exhibited a similar pattern, with the Claremont Church preparing its "red book" as a guide for understanding different interpretations of the most explicit biblical texts. North Church also produced a study booklet in which four different ways to interpret Scripture were described (see appendix number 5).

Community of Hope was perhaps the most biblically focused of the congregations. They had begun as part of the larger church with studies of parables and the reign of God. When the bishop approved the formation of a fellowship group, the people adopted a "base community" model with the regular study of Scripture as a major part of their common life. They also focused themselves on a particular text, Micah 6:8, which took on symbolic resonance as well.

Further attention was given to texts exhorting the people to reach out, serve and be "ambassadors for Christ" (2 Corinthians

144

5:16-20). The Bible was both a symbol and a regular practice of the base community, along with prayer and work for love and justice. Among the offerings was the intensive Disciple Bible Study produced by The United Methodist Church that requires a significant time commitment and regular preparation of participants. The Bible was, thus, prominent in the learning community, and, through it, Community of Hope attended to biblical themes of God's reign, God's action, and God's calling to human beings.

Epworth Church, Saratoga Springs, and Claremont were more focused on studying texts that relate to homosexuality, but they took such studies an additional step from the norm. At North, some members of the congregation wanted to reflect more thoroughly on diverse approaches to understanding homosexuality before forming their own points of view. Toward this end, the Task Force provided biblical interpretations available from the Transforming Congregation movement, a movement of churches committed to supporting homosexual persons in seeking transformation to a heterosexual orientation. Information about the Transforming Congregation movement was also provided at Epworth.

Transforming symbols. Some significant symbols of the congregations were powerful as they were reshaped. For example, an important symbol at Epworth and Claremont was the Advent wreath, which was usually lit by a "traditional" family during each Sunday in Advent. In both of these congregations different kinds of family and friendship groups were invited to light the candles. The purpose of this was made explicit at Epworth, with words about different kinds of family. The shift at Claremont was not made explicit, but happened a few months before the reconciling decision when a gay couple lit the candles in a Sunday service.

Interestingly, another transforming symbol was also connected with light—the rainbow. Both Epworth and Community of Hope congregations celebrated the rainbow as a symbol and made specific reference to the Jewish-Christian tradition of covenant, symbolized by the rainbow in the story of Noah and the flood

(Genesis 9:1-18), as well as expanded popular meanings of the rainbow in regard to race relations and inclusiveness across sexual orientation. The Community of Hope lit a rainbow candle each Sunday in worship. On one such Sunday, the leader lifted the candle and said, "Lighting this candle is a witness that in all things, we have chosen to hope rather than to curse the darkness." People often emphasize the importance of the symbols in supporting their common life, sometimes stirring conversion and new vision. The power of these light-related symbols and explicit interpretations to change people over time are considerable though subtle.

Emerging symbols. In addition to the symbols that have been described, some symbols emerged in the congregations over time. For example, Community of Hope placed a drawing of the Living Jesus, an African American interpretation, over the communion table in order to emphasize the living presence of Jesus. They later added a cross with faces of Nicaraguan people, inspired by their mission trip to Nicaragua. The same congregation developed a community banner, a remembering wall, and a companioning wall. Other congregations were less intentional about incorporating such emerging symbols, but many emerged spontaneously.

Symbolic Events. Symbolic events are also central to these congregations. Some are past events that were significant and are now part of the congregation's history and story, usually bearing meaning that surpasses the simplicity of the original experience. The Epworth story in chapter 5 begins with two stories members like to tell visitors. One is about a Filipino man who walked by the church, saw the Methodist symbol, and recognizing it, said "That's my church!" He soon became a member, along with his family and many others from the Filipino community. This man's experience began with a physical symbol, The United Methodist cross and flame, but his story became a symbolic event for the whole congregation. Without realizing it, the congregation was welcoming people through their logo. When someone from the Philippines took this welcome seriously and became part of the congregation, their self-understanding was reshaped. This is why the story is told again and again.

The founding of the Community of Hope is a similarly symbolic event, with the vision of the pastor, support of the bishop and district superintendent, and the commitment of a central group of laity. Equally symbolic for the community was the opening of a bank account in the only African American bank in Tulsa with the deposit of a check given to the pastor for conducting the funeral of a person who had died of AIDS.

Some symbolic events are sacramental celebrations. Nowhere is this more vivid that in the Community of Hope, where communion is celebrated almost every Sunday and, also, on occasion, during the week. The congregation is deeply aware of the strengthening power of Eucharist—the power of gathering as a broken people and trusting the healing that is offered in the sacrament.

Some symbolic events are ritual celebrations of life moments. The Epworth Church practices these with regularity. For example, people often host the Sunday coffee hour on their birthday or anniversary, providing refreshments for all. The congregation adds to the celebration with singing, "Happy Birthday."

Symbolic Music. Music also played a major role in many of the congregations. Community of Hope began a musical ensemble group called New Hope that sang and wrote music to embody their faith commitments toward hope and justice. The choir of the Claremont Church was one of the first groups in the congregation to integrate gay members into their full life. The choir was also a community of caring for people whose sexual orientations and points of view were diverse. This small community became a visible symbol of possibilities of inclusive ministry for other parts of the congregation in the future. At Saratoga Springs, a congregational commitment to compassion is kept alive through the continuing use of music written for the choir by Jim Borden.

Symbolic Persons. Many of the congregations also identify symbolic people. These usually included the pastor and/or one or two laypeople who gave leadership to the reconciling deliberation. In general, these people were praised by those who approved of the decision and were criticized by those who did not approve of the reconciling vote. In two of the churches, long-standing leaders of the church played major roles, each of whom had credibility in multiple contexts over time. At Saratoga Springs, Jane Borden was a major influence, and her ministry had been important to people for some time. Further, the murder of her husband, was an event that reinforced respect and compassion for Jane, as well as the memory of Jim. Even with the prominence of Jane's role, however, the RCP Task Force had deliberately distanced the pastoral staff, including her, by having a chair who was not part of the staff. This enabled the community to avoid over-identifying the issues and dialogue with particular pastoral leaders.

Lois Seifert, the person most often named at the Claremont Church was also a prominent leader, a diaconal minister who had previously been a lay member of staff and was now a very active member of the congregation. She was, in fact, an active leader of some parts of the study and dialogue process (such as the PFLAG group), but others also had leadership roles—preaching, teaching, and leading task forces and committees. Both Jane Borden and Lois Seifert were active leaders, but their symbolic leadership also seems to have been a profound dimension of their influence.

THEOLOGICAL AND ETHICAL COMMITMENTS

The primary focus of this chapter has been the dynamics of learning within the congregations. Some discussion is also needed about the influence of theological and ethical commitments of those learning patterns. Four commitments are embodied with particular clarity in the congregations of this study. The commitments are rooted in Christian doctrine and ethics, but they have taken many forms in the history of the Christian tradition. The commitments are: trust in God's grace; prophetic witness; courageous action; and communion with the congregation and the larger world.

Trust in God's grace. God's grace is a primary focus of the Christian religious tradition, and it has taken bold and explicit form in Protestant theologies. Grace also plays a central role in Wesleyan theologies, which is important to the legacy of these five congregations. John Wesley's vision for human communities was that they would live from and through the grace of God. This is made possible by their participation in the means of grace, which he understood to be the "ordinary channels" whereby God conveys grace—preventing, justifying, and sanctifying grace—to the human community. Some of these means of grace are practices instituted by God: prayer, searching the Scriptures, the Lord's Supper, fasting, and Christian conference. Other practices are "prudential means of grace," focused on particular acts of holy living and ministry (acts of charity) and daily practice of the presence of God.

Although the five congregations of this study ultimately made different decisions about their life together, all were active in practicing the means of grace. For Community of Hope, the Lord's Supper was so important that they began to practice it most Sundays, and sometimes during the week, which is more frequently than current denominational practice. For most of the congregations, prayer and study of Scripture were central. For all of them, Christian conferencing became an increasing focus over the course of their deliberations. What was described earlier as "learning in community" is a form of Christian conferencing. This took place in multiple contexts in the five congregations: worship, administrative bodies, regular classes, special study groups, and groups designated to give leadership in the reconciling deliberations. These were groups that did engage in mediating grace to one another, especially as they faced deep passions regarding sexuality and deep differences among themselves. They were turned to prayer and reflection on Scripture repeatedly, as to the discipline of learning to speak the truth in love while respecting one another in the midst of difference.

Prophetic Public Witness. One of the boldest marks of the five congregations was their passion and willingness, as congregations, to reflect theologically on pressing human concerns and to respond with prophetic public witness. Across the world, many congregations skim over such pressing concerns, making an occasional mention in pastoral prayers, sermons, or study groups. Other congregations attend to such concerns by leaving them to a small interest group while the community as a whole focuses on less controversial matters. The congregations of this study, particularly the four that continued deliberations to the point of a congregational decision, were determined to focus on issues beyond the church walls and to do so with serious, intense theological reflection, even if this meant walking through controversy. They felt called to pray for the world, to understand the world as deeply as possible, and to draw upon the best of their theological resources to analyze, critique, and respond to the world.

This approach is quite different from focusing on individual salvation and spiritual growth, although the congregations of our study actively nurtured the spiritual life of their members through worship, prayer, celebrations, conversations, and acts of care. At times, the congregations all faced tensions between internal harmony and prophetic decisions and between congregational unity and social commitment. The tension was resolved for one congregation when the senior pastor and an unofficial selection of leaders decided to suspend the discourse for the next two years.

Another sought to remove tension from their midst by arranging for a pastor to move. This was the larger congregation from which the Community of Hope emerged. Faced with tensions, most persisted because they sensed God was calling them to remain open to God's prophetic calling, wherever that might lead. For those congregations, the result has been a sharing of theological symbols, such as the cross outside the window and the rainbow, vigorous theological discourse that continues over years of living together, acceptance of diverse interpretations, and commitment to discern God's movements in the world and God's unique call for their community.

These congregations never approached prophetic action as an end in itself; it was simply the way of being faithful to the movements of God in a particular time and place. For example, all five congregations expressed a desire to move toward inclusive action without alienating or losing people. This was sometimes revealed in expressions of anxiety regarding controversy or leaving the church. It was sometimes revealed in the congregation's failure to proceed in the face of conflict. It was frequently revealed in the tension between the church's option to accept all people, including people diverse in sexual orientation, and its option to make a public announcement of this openness, including registration with the Reconciling Congregation Program. It was also revealed in the tension many people felt between their initial decision to become a Reconciling Congregation and the congregation's subsequent actions—or lack of action—to live into that decision and be transformed by it. In short, theological reflection on pressing human concerns led to action and more reflection and more action. The congregations were shaping a way of being prophetic, which included the critique and reform of their own communities.

Courageous Action. The third theological-ethical commitment of these congregations flows directly from the first two, that is, courageous action. The congregations of our study were willing to be bold if they felt called to do it. At the same time, they did not seek to act boldly and take risks for the sake of being different, although some members may have been so inclined. As a body, each of these congregations seemed determined to find ways to be in community with one another, while following through on the decisions, even risky decisions, to which they thought God was calling them. A history of courageous action seems to have prepared many of these churches for the actions they took regarding sexual orientation.

Some critical moments of courage began almost twenty years ago for Chicago's Epworth congregation, sparked by the arrival of new people. One was when the congregation had become convinced it was dying, and two dynamic sisters joined the church because they "liked what they found." They began immediately to lead the ministries of the church, and they have continued to serve in administrative positions, the shelter ministry, and other works of the church. Another critical moment was inspired by the interim pastor, Bill White, whose father had been Epworth's pastor "in the glorious past." By the time White arrived, the church had had some strong clergy and lay leadership, but was still not sure of the future. Faced with a leaky sanctuary and discouraged spirits, White reminded people that they had a choice: "You can huddle in here and die or you can open the front doors to the neighborhood and be the church of Jesus Christ in this changing neighborhood!" They chose the latter. In these two moments of courage, the Epworth Church set its course, and courage continues to be important to the dynamic ministry of the present congregation.

Over the years, the people of Epworth have made a series of courageous decisions, each contributing to a movement of courage, which has fed the prophetic public witness as well as the communion of the congregation. Each courageous action seems to have prepared them for the next, strengthening them to be more bold and to care for one another more deeply.

Communion with the Congregation and the Larger World. This discussion leads naturally to a fourth theological-ethical commitment in the five congregations—commitment to communion with the congregation and larger world. It is hardly surprising to discover that Eucharist, or communion, is a central practice in these congregations. Each congregation places high value on communion, both in the celebration of Sacraments and in the normal practices of living. Consider Epworth Church, which is marked by courage, but also by vigorous efforts to share with others in their church and larger community. The church—describing itself as "a family of followers of Jesus Christ"—values baptism and Eucharist as the community's sacraments, gathering and transforming the people. In the past two decades, Epworth has also lived sacramentally, as it has shared facilities with Ethiopian, Vietnamese, and gay charismatic congregations, and as it has served the poor of Chicago. The other congregations of this study have similar records of building internal and external community.

Commitment to communion is multilayered in all five congregations. None of these are "single-issue" congregations or even "issue-focused" congregations, however much they have been willing to wrestle with issues. These are communities that care for people and for the communities in which they live. One of the vivid testimonies to the valuing of communion is the life of

Tulsa's Community of Hope. Both in its founding and in its building as a congregation, the pastor and leaders have been intentionally communal. The original intention of the pastor was to form a community of worship and service in the world; the original vision of the bishop was to create a community informed, in part, by Latin American base communities and United Methodist Communities of Shalom. In short, this congregation was founded by people with a radical community vision, and it has continued to live into that vision ever since.

The forms of community that exist in the five congregations could be described as communities of solidarity. Even in programs for feeding hungry people and sheltering homeless people, the congregations' efforts have been hospitable, respectful, and egalitarian rather than paternalistic or condescending. These congregations have repeatedly made decisions to build the community of the church and the church's communion with the larger community, whether with the changing neighborhood, the poor of their city, or refugees who have escaped persecution in their home countries. Further, the congregations have continually criticized and reshaped their own efforts in dialogue with other people. These are congregations who are committed to communion for "the long haul," neither building an empire nor making quick responses to problems and moving on to other interests. The communal commitments—as commitments to God's grace, prophetic public witness, and courageous action—are very deep indeed!

In a world where the church has to deal with hard issues—and in a fragile world situation where both church and world are vulnerable to life-threatening forces—the insights of this chapter are very important. Christians are daily faced with threats and counterthreats of terrorist, structures of domination, and stresses imposed by modern life. In such a situation, local congregations can become combative or superficial. Human relationships can disintegrate, and relationships with God and the larger world are easily diminished. The challenge is to find more adequate ways of living in human community, which will include more adequate approaches to controversial issues. If a congregation deals with issues only in terms of win-lose debates, competition will be the primary style of relationship, issues will be the primary focus of community life, and the church community will disintegrate. If, however, a congregation chooses not to deal with hard issues, disintegration will result from superficiality and unaddressed fears, questions, yearnings, and hopes.

The church is not immune to the ways of the world. Congregations need approaches to controversy that take conflict as an invitation: to turn to God, to develop more honest and respectful relations with one another, and to consider theological and ethical commitments that are congruent with God's call in the present age. The central lesson of the congregations in this study, whether or not one agrees with their decisions, is that they have faced conflict communally and boldly. They have done so in four primary ways:

1) Facing pain and developing ministries of hospitality
2) Developing learning communities that can engage in serious dialogue and make difficult decisions
3) Allowing symbols—both traditional and emerging—to point people beyond themselves
4) Living into ever-deepening theological and ethical commitments.

Our studies suggest that congregations are most able to face controversy and make difficult decisions when they practice these multiple forms of embodied knowing. With this truism in mind, the insights of this chapter can be summarized as guidelines for congregations who long to deepen their ministries, especially in the face of seemingly overwhelming issues.

Engaging pain and ministering with hospitality. The congregations (especially the four that became reconciling) were experienced in facing pain within and without the congregation. They had experienced fire, murder, church division, near-closing of their church, homelessness on their streets, and political refugees crossing their borders. They had also experienced the movements of God's grace, stirring them into new life and min-

154

istries of new life for others. They had become story-tellers, people active in prayer and justice-making, and bearers of hope.

Building learning communities by engaging differences through dialogue. Lest this discussion sound overly ideal, we quickly observe that the congregations were, and are, messy communities where people continue to dialogue and wrestle with hard issues. Community of Hope finds itself unable to remain in a denomination that is restrictive of gay and lesbian people, choosing to leave The United Methodist Church as a matter of conscience. This has been another difficult decision for them. North's original willingness to make room for reflection about inclusion and the gospel was overpowered by biblical interpretations that foreclosed dialogue and a financial campaign for building renewal. All of the congregations point to the power of "communities of practice" in shaping a world. Some formed practices that shaped a radical new form of church (Community of Hope); some shaped a more cautious world (North); some shaped a world of ever-expanding inclusiveness (Epworth, Saratoga Springs, Claremont). They all reveal how community practices—such as participation, form giving and negotiation shape the ethos, beliefs and practices of a local congregation.

Engaging with symbols and making meaning. Through their deliberations, the five congregations have been supported and inspired by their symbols. They actively participate in these symbols, whether in celebration of Eucharist or meditation before a cross outside the window. The same symbols point them to the holy and to God's future for creation. Thus, people actively receive, interpret, and recreate their symbols, and the symbols continually lure them to glimpse God's movements in the past and God's promises for the future. We were particularly struck in our studies that symbolic people played such a prominent role. Like Martin Luther King, Jr., or Mother Teresa, certain people in the congregations seemed larger than life as congregants told their stories. On the surface, this seemed like a distortion, but we came to realize that these people had played a symbolic role; they really were signs that pointed to the congregation's story and hope. Likewise, the Bible was a powerful symbol, pointing to the past and future of God's movements, while interpreting the present life of the communities. The primary visual and musical symbols for these churches were symbols of new life and reaching out—light, rainbows, circles, artistic renderings of the living Jesus and crucified Christ, and music recalling the endless promises of God. The people of these congregations lived by hope, and they did so largely by the way they engaged anew with traditional Christian symbols and made meaning in their lives.

Living into ever-deepening theological and ethical commitments. Finally, the congregations of this study are, first and foremost, communities of faith. They are people who speak and sing their faith; who analyze, critique, and deepen their faith; who live the faith they know and actively seek to better understand their faith. This does not mean that faith for them is intellectual; rather, faith is a way of knowing that embraces every aspect of their lives. One could say that these congregations are living, by God's grace, as fully as they are able into God's call as they understand it. Other Christians will understand their calls differently, and the life patterns of the five congregations of this book will not be exactly the same for any other congregation. What is most important is simply to recognize the courage with which these communities follow what they see, continually forming and reforming their lives as they go. For these congregations, the challenges might be summarized in a few words: to trust in God's grace, to engage in prophetic public witness, to act with courage, and to live in communion with one another and the larger world. How responses to these challenges take shape in other congregations will be an adventure for the future.

Because the congregations in this study offer inspiration and guidance, we have been tempted to portray them in the best-possible light. In truth, they are simply struggling communities of ordinary people who follow the God of Life as best they can. A chapter such as this should thus conclude, not with the congregations themselves, but with the triune God whom they worship. In spite of diverse theological perspectives among and within these congregations, they finally point beyond themselves to the God who creates the cosmos and tends all of creation; to the God who redeems broken creation through the life and work of Jesus Christ; and to the God who sustains life through the ever-present Spirit blowing across the earth. We pray that the congregations of this book will, at the very least, awaken the hope that comes from God, who is the source of all true hope.

CHAPTER EIGHT

CLAIMING MINISTRIES OF COMPASSION AND JUSTICE: BEING THE BODY OF CHRIST

Deep change takes time, strategic care, patience, the conviction that we are not working alone, and the faith that there is something in the universe, as Robert Frost said, "that doesn't love a wall."

—Laurent A. Parks Daloz

CALLED TO BE THE BODY OF CHRIST

Recall a key identity story from Saratoga Springs: the cross outside the main window of the sanctuary that leads one's eye outside the walls of the church. It is the primary symbol seen and story shared with newcomers. Here is a congregation that clearly does not "love a wall." Being the Body of Christ calls the church to spend its life for the sake of the world. As John 3:16 asserts, God so loved the world that God sent Jesus. As Christ's Body, God sends us to share the good news of God's love for all, especially the poor and marginalized as Jesus' life so clearly shows.

In a classic book, *The People Called,* Paul Hanson explores the Hebrew Scriptures in depth to discover what it means to be God's called people. His work offers some key insights that lay a crucial foundation for this volume as we try to discover what it means to understand faith communities and to work toward faithful congregational change.

We are reminded in Hosea 6:1-3 of the inseparability of God's tearing and healing and in the book of Jeremiah of the inseparability of the faith of the individual and the health of the community as a whole. Both Hosea and Isaiah offer us insight into a "pedagogy of brokenness"[1] that leads to the assertion that for a community of faith to be faithful and seek to live into God's vision of justice and peace, it "must restrain and relativize all party allegiances through acknowledgment of the sole sovereignty of God."[2]

Seeking to live into such a vision is not easy. Leaders through the ages have used "God's Word" to secure their own power in and over communities. Jesus challenged religious leaders of his day who were guilty of this. All of us who have power in the church must keep our eyes on Jesus and guard against our tendencies to rationalize and to use God's Word to impose our will on the church. We all "know only in part, and we prophesy only in part" (1 Corinthians 13:9). All who would be leaders in the Body of Christ must offer leadership with openness and humility.

All of us, when we are honest with ourselves, struggle with personal and social dilemmas that keep us awake at night. We, like the psalmists before us, argue with God and beg for God to "make it plain." And then—when we are sure that it is plain—we run the risk of an arrogance that judges us. Even so, we feel certain that on some issues we truly do understand God's will and way. Yet, we are confronted with sisters and brothers in faith who are sure that exactly the opposite is most certainly God's will and way. How are we to become a grounded community of called out

160

people who seek to live both faithfully and prophetically in a world so divided, diverse, and out of control?

If we are to live as the Body of Christ in ways that grow out of the Hebraic understanding of a called people, our life together must be "grounded in the God of mystery whose presence faithfully guides all worlds to their final goal." We must practice "treating every opinion honestly and fairly with a freedom rooted in communion with the ultimate Reality, in whom all polarities find their final rest."[3] How this is done is the dilemma addressed in this chapter.

In the early Yahwistic tradition, there are three interlocking characteristics of what it means to be God's faithful, called out people:

1) Community as response to God's initiating saving activity;
2) Devotion to the one true God as the unifying heart of community; and
3) Community defined by the triad of righteousness, compassion, and worship.[4]

Grounding our exploration of how congregations learn compassion and commitment based on a biblical understanding of "called out community" is an important foundation for our work. The plea of Ephesians 4:1-6 resonates with the Hebrew understanding of the people of God:

> I therefore, the prisoner in the Lord, beg you to lead a life worthy of the calling to which you have been called, with all humility and gentleness, with patience, bearing with one another in love, making every effort to maintain the unity of the Spirit in the bond of peace. There is one body and one Spirit, just as you were called to the one hope of your calling, one Lord, one faith, one baptism, one God and Father of all, who is above all and through all and in all.

The purpose of this chapter is to revisit the narratives to see how these congregations were able or not able to work together in humility and gentleness and with patience and love. In what ways were they able or not so able to "maintain the unity of the Spirit in the bond of peace"? What helped them live into "the one hope of [their] calling"? What kinds of processes or issues blocked this goal?

A CALL TO CHANGE

In the last chapter we examined events that challenged the status quo and provided impetus for these congregations to re-examine their identity and story as a particular people of God and what it means to be faithful to that identity. Each of the congregations had some event or person who introduced cognitive dissonance that demanded response. Questions were raised, pain was acknowledged, silences were broken. In most cases, participants can look back and name these events or share stories that embody the birth or rejection of their congregation's journey toward the possibility of change.

A recognition that we need to change does not occur in a vacuum. It grows out of our history. Sometimes our sense of history and identity impels us to change; sometimes it impedes our ability to respond in risky and unknown ways. If we are to risk deep change in the church, we have to ground our faith communities in integrated worship, compassion, and justice. Then, when an event or a person introduces cognitive dissonance into the congregation by raising questions or challenging assumptions, we will have the trust and security to explore difficult questions together. Doing this requires that we open ourselves to multiple perspectives that both challenge and stretch our comfort zones. It means that we must learn to live with paradox and mystery.

Eric Law calls Christians to create "margins of grace" where people who enjoy the safety and security of knowing they belong, and those who find themselves outside a given community and living at the mercy of their fears, can come together on neutral turf.[5] When people dare to step into this borderland space between safety and fear and work together to speak truthfully and listen with empathy, communities (and individuals) have the potential to become more inclusive and just.

A call to change can spark controversy with lightning speed. Though we examined the process of congregations who were exploring the possibility of opening their doors in public ways to gay, lesbian, transgendered, and bisexual persons, controversy in communities comes in many guises. We hear about congregations deeply divided over issues ranging from Sunday morning worship and education schedules, to how often and in what way communion is to be celebrated, to inclusive language, to the role of women in church leadership, to whether or not to relocate. Congregations struggle with issues of racial inclusiveness, over sharing leadership with new and younger members, and even over when and by whom the silver service can be used!

Any issue which has the potential of dividing a congregation and diverting it from its mission and ministry in and for the world is a serious issue. The insights in this chapter come from the congregations we studied, real people with real issues. Their ways of creating space where genuine dialogue could occur can help both clergy and lay leaders of congregations handle issues that call forth strong emotional reactions. Their learning offers ways to deal fairly and openly with whatever has the potential to divide and divert the church from faithful discipleship in the world.

Congregations are called to "mindful learning" which invites the creation of new categories.[6] Mindful learning invites us to be open to the possibility that there is more than one right answer. This is not easy for people or communities that have a long history of resting secure in the way things have always been—or, at least, presumed to be.

Opening one's mind or a community to the possibility of genuine dialogue can be painful. It takes time. Creating environments where persons feel safe to share, to disagree, and to risk is crucial. Laurent Daloz suggests inviting people to "let air under their assumptions" by considering "what if . . ." and "suppose that . . ." as one way of considering new ways to thinking and seeing without having to let go of current beliefs.[7] Perhaps, having tried an idea out and played with it for a while, people may be ready and able to change at some point in the future. How can we create such environments and processes?

Creating a safe environment includes an awareness of the way we talk to each other. Propositional statements invite debate rather than dialogue. They interject the possibility of winning and losing. Too often, instead of listening to understand, we are listening in order to form our rebuttal so we can persuade or even put down the speaker.

On the other hand, personal stories and "I" statements invite empathy and questions. For instance, members of the Reconciling Congregation Task Force at Saratoga Springs prefaced their comments with the phrase, "I have come to believe that . . ." Empathy leads toward connected, relational ways of knowing.[8] This requires listening to understand and developing empathy-seeking to see through another's eyes. Jack Mezirow asserts that "feelings of trust, solidarity, security, and empathy are essential preconditions for free full participation in discourse." Without trust persons have little tolerance for living with "paradox, searching for synthesis, and reframing."[9]

How did the congregations in our study create environments that allowed them to engage in real dialogue and explore the possibilities of change? For the Claremont, Epworth, and Saratoga Springs congregations, there was already a history of working on and living into prophetic and justice-seeking ministries. Whether the issue was inclusive language, creating a homeless shelter, or becoming a sanctuary church, there was a history and a sense that "we've done this before and we can do it again now." For these three congregations, the Reconciling Congregation study had a possible positive outcome because many members already perceived that "this is who we are."

Trust is not something that comes quickly. It requires time, openness, and a sense that it is safe to see things differently and to speak about these differences. It also requires the perception that there are no hidden agendas or even competing agendas. Saratoga Springs demonstrated the power of being intentional about using "I" statements so that people named and claimed their own experiences and ideas and avoided attacking others and their views. They learned the importance of this kind of candor from an earlier unsuccessful attempt to introduce the Reconciling Congregation Program. A perception in the congregation that there was a hidden agenda undermined the trust needed to proceed at that time.

Two of the things that seemed to work against building trust at North were the mixed messages sent by the senior pastor and the strong pressure from those who did not want anything to impede their agenda of raising almost three million dollars to renovate and add to the physical plant. Behind-the-scenes meetings of ad hoc groups also undermined the process at North.

The biggest factor undermining trust in each of the congregations seemed to be fear. At North, it was fear that the building campaign would suffer. For some people and families in each of the congregations, it was fear "for their children" or that somehow their "biblical faith" was being undermined. Too often, this fear appears in the form of an underlying anxiety that cannot be named or examined, but is a powerful deterrent to trust. Fear when it is named and acknowledged can be addressed. Even though people may not—and probably will not—all come to agree, there can be a sense that everyone was heard, that their voices and opinions were received as honest statements and reflections of their faith, and that the family of faith can survive honest differences. This seemed to be the case for most in the Epworth congregation.

It must be acknowledged, however, that some people who were able to engage paradox and to examine all sides of the issue made considered judgments that their understanding of Scripture or their concern for their children would not allow them to remain in a community that decided to publicly say that they welcomed homosexual persons. Two of the people who left Epworth clearly fall into this category. Their leaving caused pain for both them and the small congregation but everyone acknowledged that sometimes faith journeys diverge and each must go on in ways that have integrity for them. Learning when to take leave and giving those who take leave a blessing as they go is part of what it means to be faithful Christian communities.

As Mezirow observes, because our "values and sense of self . . . are often emotionally charged," they will be defended with energy and strength. Our values and sense of self, or "frames of reference . . . provide us with a sense of stability, coherence, community, and identity."[10] In Christian communities, a frame of reference—such as how we understand and interpret Scripture—has both moral and social implications. It also has implications for how we learn and how we live together in community. Congregations will be helped to attend to the challenges of dealing with change if they recognize and are attentive to their particular frames of reference.

Some communities will decide that to be faithful means not to be more inclusive, but to hold fast to their beliefs about Scripture and morality. As other faith communities move toward creating a more inclusive frame of reference in response to Scripture and morality as they understand it, they will open themselves to multiple points of view that both challenge and stretch the boundaries of individual members and congregations.

It seems clear from the congregations we studied that the process of change is very different for large program-driven congregations and for smaller, faith-family congregations. This insight has many implications for how pastors and lay leaders function in every aspect of congregational leadership. For example, in a small congregation like Epworth, everyone knew and respected the members who believed it would not be faithful for the congregation to become a Reconciling Congregation. In their discussions they continued to love and care about one another in spite of differences on the issue of homosexuality. Everyone tried to "fight fair" and to avoid personal attack even when they were passionate about the beliefs being shared. They recognized pain in themselves and in others, on both sides of the issue at hand.

At Epworth, it was their practice to have a guest preacher and then remain in the sanctuary for a time of questions and discussion at the close of the service. Another strategy was to print a list of people who would be glad to have a private conversation with anyone who did not want to speak or ask questions at the public gatherings. Everyone in the congregation knew on a first name basis someone on the list.

In contrast, at North, with 1,100 members, and Saratoga Springs, with 800 members, a relatively small percentage of those large congregations were actively involved in the study and decision-making process. Apart from sermons preached and information in the church newsletter and in the weekly bulletin at worship, many were on the periphery or completely outside the educational efforts to inform and challenge people to support change.

Unlike Saratoga Springs and North, at Epworth no one chose to speak for or against the issue at the time the vote was taken. In that small congregation opinions and the pain of knowing about the differences were already in the open for all to see. They had already dealt openly and painfully with the issues involved and all were ready to vote.

Tactics—like calling in the press on the night of the vote and maneuvering behind the scenes—were used in the large congregations that would not have been tolerated in a small, close community like those at Epworth and the Community of Hope. This is not to say that no small community would use similar tactics. But to the extent that small congregations function as healthy families, this type of behavior is less likely to occur. There, people have agreed to disagree.

While valiant efforts were made to reach everyone in all of the congregations, not all chose to participate or simply did not decide to participate. The decision, which at North was meant by the Task Force to be a transitional decision in an envisioned continuing process, was made by the official bodies of the congregation and through behind-the-scenes negotiation in a quasi-official group. Although there were educational opportunities in various settings and formats, crucial decisions and compromises were made by a few powerful leaders. Finally, the decision-making process subverted the carefully planned two-year long educational process.

In contrast, the Claremont congregation acknowledged disagreement and pain on both sides of the issue. The pastor tried to be fair and open to all parishioners while offering clear, prophetic leadership. The voting was a weeklong process using secret ballots so that every effort was made to invite every church member to vote. For a congregation with about 500 members, this was a long, patient, and pains-taking process.

At Saratoga Springs, the congregational vote at a Church Conference became a celebratory and life-changing event for many. The media, invited by one who feared the change, was welcomed and the culmination of the process seemed to have positive and energy-generating results. Possibly more important, there was a level of trust running through the congregation that made it possible for people who may not agree with the Reconciling Congregation decision to know that they are still welcome there, too. Many who might have left at that time did not because it is clear to them that there is room for many perspectives at Saratoga Springs.

The situation at Community of Hope differs in many ways from the other four congregations. In this community, the questions were not about including those who have been marginalized by the church for this was a community of the marginalized. The issues of trust and fear they had to wrestle with were not about themselves as a faith community; rather, they were about how far they might dare to trust The United Methodist Church and its representatives.

Their issues also involved how much they should put their pastor and her ministerial credentials at risk. Their decision to disaffiliate with The United Methodist Church after the 1996 General Conference was seen as a necessity for their integrity as a Christian community. Sometimes risking change calls Christians to acts of courage that go far beyond where they ever imagined they might be going.

CLAIMING MINISTRIES OF COMPASSION AND JUSTICE

The narratives about these five congregations include considerable detail about how each congregation claimed ministries of compassion and justice over long periods of time. We offer the following guidelines and cautions for congregations where people feel called to risk change for the sake of the gospel.

Be attentive to a congregation's context and history. Seek to build on strengths and to acknowledge fears and leftover pain from the past.

Name issues clearly and stay with the issue for the long haul. Commit to "no more silence, no more tears" and be patient and tenacious in staying the course. Do not foreclose discussions of potentially explosive issues because it is painful. Stay with the pain even as Jacob wrestled all night with the angel.

Allow plenty of time and extend it if the "time is not yet." Processes that involve deeply held beliefs require time. Some who believe the time to act is long past will be frustrated. Others will never be ready to face the issue and act. Leaders must lead a process in which the community has a voice about when the time has come.

Honor pastoral/leadership decisions to extend the time of exploration. It is important to extend the time of exploring issues involved in a difficult decision so that whatever decision is made will have as broad a base in the community as a whole as possible. Seek unity and minimize having winners and losers. Simply squeaking by under "the letter of the law" does not build up a community of faith. At Epworth the pastor made a decision that was supported by the community to require a two-thirds affirmative vote for the decision to become a Reconciling Congregation to pass.

Develop strategies that foster dialogue. Recognize that this requires honesty, safety, and the ability to respond with empathy to those who differ. It requires that ways be found to invite and listen to those who often find themselves without a voice. This was done at North in the session where gay and lesbian members of the congregation talked about their experience as persons without a voice in The United Methodist Church due to inhospitable church policies.

Create safe and hospitable space where personal stories can be told and heard. It is not possible for a congregation to learn to respect a variety of perspectives unless members have firsthand experience with sharing stories and hearing stories from people whose life journeys differ from their own. Allow space for differing opinions and the naming of both fears and hopes. Honor anger and tears as appropriate responses to speaking and hearing the truth in love.

Invite, frame and reframe questions so multiple points of view are fostered. Find ways to help people recognize that there is more than one right answer. Be prepared to explain that everyone will bring their own stories and fears to the table when a congregation explores and risks change. Empathy depends on helping people learn how to see their story and their fears from the point of view of others in the group.

Create a leadership team that includes clergy and laity. Regardless of the issue related to possible change in a congregation, all constituencies should be represented in the leadership team that initially explores the issues and develops strategies to educate the congregation about the issues. Whether the leadership team is appointed, elected, or voluntary, someone should attempt to ensure broad representation that includes attention to age, race, gender, class, and theological perspective and various roles in the congregation. A broad-based leadership team is essential if people in the congregation are going to feel valued, included, and invested in the process and its outcomes.

As we have lived with and pondered the stories of these congregations we have identified a list of characteristics found in various leaders in the congregations. Being a leader as suggested below leaves room for people of all ages and perspectives to assume leadership roles. No one will embody all of these roles or characteristics. However, every congregation has people who embody some of these roles. When change is pursued, calling forth the various gifts of many different members is what it means to be the Body of Christ. Learning to recognize and call forth the gifts of many in the community is one of the most important roles of congregational leaders.

Clergy and lay leaders in congregations can foster growth and change in individuals and congregations when they are attentive to the following aspects of leadership for change:

- Offering a vision
- Creating a margin of grace
- Listening to all in nonjudgmental ways
- Inviting people into new life in Jesus Christ
- Living faithfully themselves
- Embodying justice, mercy, and humility
- Honoring diversity
- Designing inclusive processes
- Inviting dialogue
- Staying with the issue when the going gets tough
- Being patient
- Naming differing realities
- Offering fresh images and new metaphors and stories
- Risking for the sake of the gospel
- Willing to sit at the foot of the table
- Walking into their own pain
- Acknowledging the pain of others
- Framing and reframing questions
- Recognizing when the time is right to act
- Taking responsibility for outcomes and follow-up
- Sharing praise

CONNECTING COMPASSION, JUSTICE, AND WORSHIP

For all of the congregations in this study, worship is at the heart of the community. Sermons were powerful as preachers dared to consider seeing and thinking in new ways. Sharing at the Lord's Table with gay and straight together attested to a unity that is greater than sexual orientation. Engaging in ritual acts—like Don and Alan lighting the Advent candles as a family or Peter reading the part of Jesus in the passion narrative on Palm Sunday at Epworth—touched people's hearts.

171

Naming pain and challenging worshipers to widen the circle to embody the kind of inclusiveness Jesus lived were proclaimed from pulpits in all five congregations. There was a desire to act justly in all five congregations. Yet, as indicated by the experi-ence of these congregations, it is a long process that leads from good intentions to something approximating congregational una-nimity about this particular justice ministry. We found several common forms of resistance to a public declaration of reconcili-ation with all kinds of people. The question asked most often about becoming a Reconciling Congregation was, "Why do we have to put a sign out front?" or "Why do we have to be so pub-lic about it?" Another form of avoidance was the tendency in sev-eral of the congregations to point out an existing justice ministry, such as feeding the hungry, as if to say, "Why would we need more than one justice ministry?"

Some people were able to acknowledge feeling compassion for gay and lesbian persons in the community but were unable to make a connection between personal acceptance and the public nature of the justice claim espoused by Reconciling Congregation advocates. The experience of the congregations that eventually became Reconciling Congregations seems to indicate that feeling and expressing compassion for individuals is a prior step to being able to name heterosexism as a public justice issue that the gospel compels congregations to speak out against. Congregations continue to need help in finding connections between the gospel's twin calls to compassion and justice.

Paul Hanson argues persuasively that healthy faith communi-ties rest on three legs:—integrated worship, compassion, and the seeking of justice. All congregations must find ways to hold these in critical and creative tension in order to live the gospel as the Body of Christ if they are to be faithful. Hanson eloquently states this conviction in the closing pages of his book, *The People Called.*

> It is in the vast choir of witnesses to God's presence in our world that the message is proclaimed that a people is God's people not when it copies a past polity or perpetuates its own

image, but when, guided by its scriptural and confessional heritage, it glimpses God's presence in the world, and responds faithfully to that presence in confession, worship, and action. For that glimpse and that response have constituted the true community of faith through all ages. They form the heart of its transcendent vision.[11]

CHAPTER NINE

CONGREGATIONS REFORMED AND RENEWED: THE BROKEN-YET-MADE-WHOLE BODY OF CHRIST

The broken-yet-made-whole chalice is a metaphor for transformational living and learning. Its sense of brokenness, yet its promise of wholeness, reflects the ongoing paradox and dynamic of being. It graphically depicts a central truth of Christian faith: "If you lose your life you will find it." It holds within it both emptiness and fullness. It embodies the truth about everyday contemporary life yet intersects that experience with Christian stories of the death and resurrection of Jesus Christ. It is a powerful reminder of the heritage and tradition of Christian faith that has been reformed in the past and continues to be reformed in the present. It embraces the tension that exists between traditional and newly emerging Christian values. It beckons from the Table—always there to sustain but also, to challenge.

When this symbol came into the life of the Community of Hope it resonated at a deep level with the purpose and mission the community sought to claim. The community adopted it because it represented much of what they knew about their own lives and the affirmation they were hungry to hear from Christian faith. It represented their own brokenness and woundedness yet also the strengths, skills, and gifts they discovered in themselves, often beyond what they had known. Like all good metaphors the broken-yet-made-whole chalice was a tool for "trying to comprehend partially what cannot be comprehended totally."[1] It invited them to imagine, as described in a church brochure, what life could be like when "in community, as the love and grace of God works in and through us, we are empowered to claim both our brokenness and our giftedness, so that together we can be and do more than anyone of us can be or do alone."

This became reality as people who felt marginalized were empowered for ministry. So many who were sick or suffering oppression and rejection found a sense of healing and empowerment when they were able to reach out together to recognize and respond to the suffering of others. The oppressed were empowered for ministry. This experiment in Christian community became a way of knowing and learning. The broken-yet-made-whole chalice created a bridge between the ability to talk about and address pain and suffering and the ability of a congregation to engage potentially divisive issues as a group. It became a holding center around which leadership could provide a safe environment for disagreement and honesty.

Above all, it was when gathered around the table on which the chalice was placed in worship that the community began to know itself as a particular kind of community—one of hospitality, of shared narratives, of journeying together, of seeking justice. Worship became central for transformation as a community and as individuals. As stories were shared, many experienced a new sense of self-acceptance. As individuals told their stories within the context and confidentiality of worship—during the time for joys and concerns—they rehearsed being a community that listened, that welcomed, that accepted and included people who had experienced rejection. This experience was often described by members as something real—an experience in which "something is at stake, that the church is making a very tangible difference in people's lives." Through their worship together, they came to know that they embodied the love and acceptance of Jesus Christ for each other.

THE BROKEN-YET-MADE-WHOLE CHALICE AS A METAPHOR

Transformational learning is similar to the meanings signified by the broken-yet-made-whole chalice. Transformational learning requires identifying individual brokenness in community and taking the risk of facing it together. Transformational learning includes moving through the dynamics of exile, sanctuary, hospitality, compassion, discipleship, and solidarity. It means that people are able to experience themselves as being lost and being found. These dynamics provide clarity in understanding the different aspects of transformational risk taking that undergird individual and communal commitment to a prophetic lifestyle with hope.

While these dynamics may be somewhat less obvious in the congregations that eventually joined the Reconciling Congregation Program, each of them also experienced suffering and loss, as individuals and as communities. At Saratoga Springs, the shocking and inexplicable murder of a beloved pastor created a need for mutual compassion and a new sense of solidarity between congregation and staff. At Claremont, "speaking the truth in love" during a prolonged period of corporate soul-searching was a painful experience for everyone, regardless of point of view. Yet the care and compassion with which they moved through a learning process that shattered certainties for many led over time to a newfound and deepened solidarity with people suffering injustice and with each other. At Epworth, the shock of realizing that one group within the family-like congregation deeply objected to a public policy of inclusiveness for moral and theological reasons required renewed commitment to mutual understanding with compassion. They learned that the mercy and compassion they offered so well to "outsiders" was needed within as well as without.

In each congregation, it was an experience of suffering together that loosened the community's sense of cohesiveness enough to create a sense of exile, a shared need for sanctuary. As these congregations struggled to see themselves and each other in new ways, they found new compassion for each other, a different grasp of the meaning of discipleship, and eventually, the excitement of moving forward into a different future together. A similar transformation never took place at North where the process of carefully exploring a commitment to inclusiveness was short-circuited by the presence of a small group of powerful leaders with a competing agenda, the expansion and renovation of the church building. The carefully planned educational design never got to the point of learning to work through the disagreement and tension that are a part of making a difficult group decision. This suggests that a capacity to support each other in working and living through the tension and uncertainty of making a difficult and potentially alienating decision is necessary if new meanings and symbols are to emerge from the process of exploration.

From the beginning the congregations that risked facing differences and conflict were encouraged to think theologically and to rework theology. Transformational learning occurred when they were open to the intersection between life events and constructing meaning in relation to stories embodied in the wisdom of the Christian faith. This is obvious at Saratoga Springs where the congregation had already spent nearly ten years dealing with differences about the use of inclusive language in worship. Claremont, with the support of the pastor, accepted thinking theologically as part of its ongoing heritage. Epworth and Community of Hope had pastors who continually modeled with intentionality this aspect of discernment. At Saratoga Springs, during their period of preparation for congregational decision making, there were three different adult education series about how to interpret the Bible. Members learned that the Bible is a rich enough resource to support a reworking of theology without fear. We concluded that the ability to rework theology is a central dynamic of transformative learning.[2] This reworking of theology was dependent on stories, symbols, rituals, and ideas that were rich enough to allow the construction of new cultural patterns and practices.

The social dynamics of change influence the internal life and social witness of Christian communities. These dynamics have within them fear and anxiety. Fear closes down learning, especially creative processes. We know from brain research that experiences of fear and anxiety actually change the structure of the brain. When threatened or feeling stress, the brain "downshifts" into that part of the brain that focuses on physical survival. At times like this, creative processes are affected and learning is reduced and limited. Environments that are perceived as unsafe can stifle creative problem solving and thinking. Relaxed and safe environments where there is challenge, but not threat, foster the use of the capacity of the whole brain.[3] A relaxed and safe environment that undergirds challenge was already a part of the prior experience of the congregations that were able to stay with the exploration process despite events that threatened to shut them down. At Epworth and Claremont, vocal opposition could have short-circuited their intention to discuss the issues thoroughly before making a decision. At Saratoga Springs, vocal opposition cropped up just before the decision was to be made at a congregational meeting. In a congregation with less experience and confidence about moving through fear, the meeting might have been canceled.

Learning involves taking risks, and fear often accompanies risk taking. We found that all of these congregations were willing to take risks; and in doing so, all had to deal with a fair amount of fear and anxiety. Prophetic dimensions often create anxiety. There were numerous contexts and issues that contributed to fear and anxiety. There was fear from violence and physical threats. There was fear of further rejection, fear of being unfaithful to a held tradition, fear of being co-opted by the institutional church, fear of alienating and losing members, fear of jeopardizing the credentials of a pastor, fear of cautions from the center, and fear of freedom from the margins, fear of keeping boundaries tight, and fear of pushing boundaries. Taking risks did incur anxiety, fear, and hurt.

We remember the story of Peter and other disciples in the boat, alarmed by an apparition coming across the lake toward them. The "ghost" turned out to be Jesus. Peter was invited by Jesus to walk with him on the water. Peter stepped out, took a few steps, realized what he was doing, and began to sink.

How were these congregations enabled to "keep their eyes on Jesus" as they risked "walking on the water"? How did they deal with the tension between their initial prophetic decisions and their subsequent actions to live into the decision and to let themselves be challenged by it? One factor affecting risk taking in these congregations, and identified in other similar studies, includes a strong congregational commitment to an identifiable mission in which many members participate. In almost every case these commitments include a passion to address social injustice in some form. At Claremont, the long-term congregational commitment to justice ministries was surely a major factor in sustaining an exploration process of nearly ten years duration before making a decision about joining the Reconciling Congregation Program.

Congregations that do not flee from the anxiety of undertaking a challenging congregational study process learn that living with uncertainty about outcome and the pain of disagreeing with friends and respected leaders can—in God's grace and in God's good time—lead to new understandings of prophetic ministry, healing, and hope. The "wounded healer" reminds us that hurt and fear can be accompanied by hope and healing.[4] Living with ambiguity can be accepted as normal and necessary rather than something out of the ordinary.

TRANSFORMATION AND LEARNING STRATEGIES

While books have been written about congregations characterized as "learning" congregations, the following discussion includes descriptions of learning strategies for change used specifically to prepare a congregation to make a difficult, anxiety-producing decision. In the congregations we studied in-depth, there were many examples of structured, semistructured and unstructured ways of knowing and learning as well as spontaneous and planned circles of interaction. Special classes and studies were offered in short-term and long-term settings. The interplay between resources available to a congregation and the openness and imagination of the congregation and its leaders to draw upon those resources influenced direction as did the congregation's inherited identity. Task Forces were formed with assignments to explore issues, design learning strategies and report back to official bodies. Sermons were preached using Scripture lessons that spoke to the issues at hand and to the life events of members.

There were safe places to gather information, hear stories, ask questions, share lives, and consider different perspectives. And there were simple moments involving people who embodied the issues in specific ways that influenced the congregation's understanding. There was the interplay between denominational activities and local church movements. Each congregation was influenced by denominational policies and by the actions and attitudes of regional bodies like the Annual Conference.

In these congregations the development of empathy and compassion was a major aspect of the power of the learning strategies, both those that were planned and those that were spontaneous. Getting to know each other in the activities of the congregation, whether it be choir, teaching Sunday school, or church commissions—as individuals sharing life experience— was key in many of these communities. The quiet influence of simple moments had great impact.

Actual engagement in ministries that served others who were hurting and oppressed strengthened relationships between the congregations and their communities. In both environments— church and community—relationships in which there was tacit permission to risk sharing pain and to risk being present to that pain opened a willingness to want to know and understand others different from themselves. An empathic kind of knowing came from seeing pain in the eyes of another, hearing their stories, and engaging in work together. This empathic knowing of "the other" led to compassion, a key element in transformative learning.

Another key element in transformative learning is the ability of leaders to enable the community to learn to think theologically and to participate in reworking theology. In addition to helping people become self-conscious about biblical interpretation, hearing how personal stories are intersected by biblical stories, teaching in Bible study groups and sermons encouraged people to make connections between their own stories and biblical stories. When the pastors in our study used metaphorical thinking in relation to biblical stories and particular events in the life of a congregation, they facilitated group potential for theological reflection and for reworking theology. The extensive use of symbols and metaphors by the pastors of these congregations also modeled a way of creating meaning that moves away from overly literal interpretations of the Bible.

Transformative learning also involves learning to question assumptions. There were questions as basic as "What is the church?" or "What is marriage?" There were questions as challenging as "Why do we think of God only as masculine?" An atmosphere that opened thinking encouraged questions and critique; it permitted people to express their discomfort with a new approach. Critical thinking about conventional attitudes and practices was necessary but was introduced in ways that allowed differences and did not insist that everyone must agree or conform. The choir director who told people they could sing either new inclusive language or the traditional words in the hymnal during worship is an example of giving people space during a process of change. The congregations learned to see in new ways and to realize that there is truth to be found in each way of seeing. In time, people were willing to risk naming and examining their own assumptions and to consider whether or not they needed to be altered. These are some of the ways that congregations engaged the hard work of open, ongoing dialogue, even when it was painful.

The strongest examples of this reworking of theology and how this reworking took place are found in the creation and adoption of symbols within those communities. In addition to the broken-yet-made-whole chalice there was the "not-quite-round" communion table. There was the translucent candle with a rainbow and Shalom that was identified as the Christ candle. There was the cross from Nicaragua on which faces of people from that country were carved. There was the companioning wall of handprints, the braided rug, the cross outside the window, the base community, sanctuary. In each case the symbols gave materiality and visibility to the commitments of the community, served as the memory of the community, and provided an ongoing unforgettable foundation for continuing reflection and extension of those commitments.

These learning experiences and the symbols that embodied them were integral to movement toward wholeness for the congregation as a group, as well as for individuals. In four of the congregations prophetic action contributed to healing as healing contributed to prophetic action. Learning that transforms lives and congregations not only confronts brokenness but also moves toward wholeness. Evidence of wholeness is found in the many ways through which that learning occurred:

- Narrative and story
- Pain and rejection
- Empathy and compassion

- Dialogue and conversation
- Ministry to hurting people
- Reflection about prophetic action

Transformative learning takes time. At North, the abrupt termination of the learning process robbed people of the opportunity to learn and experience the kind of empathy needed to sustain discussions of different points of view when a congregation is making a difficult decision. The senior pastor at North called the educational process the finest design he had ever seen. As in the other congregations, the design incorporated many kinds of learning—empathic, experiential, artistic, cognitive, paradoxical, hospitality, spatial, logical, incarnational. Yet, without some shared group goal—like making an important decision about congregational identity—the most sophisticated educational design rarely leads to transformation. The kind of transformative learning that changes people and congregations occurs in an environment where there is some tension but not so much that people withdraw in fear.[5]

CHARACTERISTICS OF A CONGREGATION ENGAGED IN TRANSFORMATIVE LEARNING

A learning, risking community of faith remembers its history, is clear about present identity, and calls forth, both corporately and personally, a vision of hope. Learning, risking congregations have the capacity to learn to hear differing voices, to converse, and to seek to understand why each one says what they do. They are willing to risk naming and examining their own assumptions and to consider whether or not they need to be altered. Such congregations regard the hard work of open, ongoing dialogue—even when it is painful—as integral to their ongoing life and mission as Christians. For instance, the leaders of the Reconciling Congregation process at Saratoga Springs and Claremont were committed to engaging as many members of the congregation as possible in that particular risky exploration.

Another factor integral to transformative learning is the role of the pastor in giving leadership, inspiring the congregation through sermons and teaching, consciousness-raising, and giving pastoral support to people with diverse experiences and beliefs. That pastor's leadership style, steadiness in relation to people and issues, pastoral sensitivities to ambivalence and change are influential. The pastor must have the ability to create a safe environment for disagreement and honesty, to create a holding center, to frame and reframe issues, and to encourage imagination. Also, transformative learning environments are created when the pastor offers partnership, when pastors inspire rather than coerce. They empower, enabling a congregation to utilize and access the knowledge and skills of all, using conflict to creatively arrive at solutions that go beyond compromise to actualize new possibilities. The direct involvement of the pastor—or senior pastor—in a process like consideration of RCP membership probably depends on the size of the congregation. Even if the pastor is not directly involved in this process, he or she must be comfortable with risk and change if the congregation is going to be capable of considering a decision that has the potential to transform them.

But equally as important is the commitment of laity, sometimes only a small core of leadership, who are willing to enter into this sense of partnership as well, who recognize and honor the complexity of the role of the pastor as a valued leader, and who have the ability to engage in mutual respect and peaceful conflict resolution over the long haul. These laity have a vision and sense of Christian community rather than a therapeutic orientation bent on securing individual needs, personal agendas, and quick fixes.

Congregations engaged in transformational learning have the ability to take charge of their own learning and a desire to discern more clearly the common ministry to which they are called. This is nurtured by leaders like the pastor at Saratoga Springs, who described his role as that of a facilitator-resource person who helped launch new groups in his congregation when a need for a group was brought to his attention by laity. He had no need to meet with or direct a new group on a continuing basis, an attitude that fostered leaders capable of taking charge of their own learning. His hands-off practice contributes to the extent to which there is continuous learning through reflection on ministry experiences in various groups in the congregation. This was also encouraged by the extent to which he and his predecessors there had engaged Scripture in worship and study as a continuous source of insight, inspiration, and guidance about the faith journey of the congregation over a long period of time.

Education is often imaged as classes in which knowledge is transferred from a teacher to a class, especially to a class of children or young people. Our study indicates that transformative learning is a more holistic image of education for communities of faith. Moving the focus away from programs and classes to an understanding of the many ways that people can participate in their own learning and formation as Christians can radically change the way we think about education in the church. When we associate Christian education primarily with a standard series of classes for each age group we try to improve our programs by finding the right curriculum materials and teachers who can implement these materials effectively. This reduces the rich, broad process of faith formation to a one-dimensional process in which the learner, be it child, teen or adult, is reduced to the familiar role of passive consumer of goods and services.

An image that emerges from asking about the relationship between education and decision making in congregations suggests that education is what happens when members of the faith community engage together in sharing their stories and questions in light of the stories embraced by the Christian tradition. For adults and teens, an important source of stories and questions is reflection together on their shared practice of ministry. In writing about change in the church, Loren Mead observes that, "We are not dealing with something that is responsive to a new program—even a very good program. We are engaged in a basic interaction between religious institutions and the nature of our social environment. . . . We do not need a new set of programs. We need churches with a new consciousness of themselves and their task."[6]

The experience of these congregations reveals that much education occurs when problems are identified and engaged, when persons of the community reflect together on their experiences of ministry, when members of the congregation know themselves to be cocreators of the congregation's evolving culture and participants in the sharing of its decisions and life, engaging together in the shared practice of ministry. This is an education that focuses not on mastery but on connection and solidarity.

This is learning that includes instruction but is much broader than the simple mastery of knowledge about the Christian tradition. Transformative learning is composed of a network of multi-layered dynamics that join liturgy, proclamation, sharing of joys and concerns, the practice of spiritual disciplines, community discernment, and involvement in mission and service in the world. Christian education occurs when all members of a faith community are welcome at the Table—both for dialogue and Eucharist—and are expected to engage mind, heart, and body as together this community of faith addresses the hard questions at hand.

This kind of learning is similar to characteristics of what Thomas Hawkins calls a learning congregation:

> Congregations become long-term communities that are the context for fundamental change. They are the places where people expect continuous learning, growing, changing, transformation.
>
> Leaders of such communities foster continuous learning and support ongoing growth. Their members continually learn to do new things and constantly challenge the assumptions behind why and how they do what they do. They are equipped to think more complexly, to clarify the mental maps that guide their thinking and acting, and to discern ever more clearly the common ministry to which God calls them through Jesus Christ. These congregations have an open flow of communication that encourages the free movement of ideas and information. They are characterized by theologically informed members and by leaders who understand themselves as shaping meaning in a community of shared practice.[7]

In this book about congregational change, we have described in considerable detail a process of education and decision making toward change that occurred in only one moment of the history of these congregations. But we also know that if congregations are to continue to make faithful change they have to continue to aspire to greater complexity in the way they compose reality.[8]

Being truly present to those who are different changes expectations of internal homogeneity so familiar to most congregations to "a corporate unity that can include a robust pluralism within. Such churches are places where . . . we come to learn to 'stand each other.' This means the community learning to understand itself. . . . It is not called, at least initially, for warm compatibility and harmony. Rather, members are called into honest struggle with each other, and in dialogue with Scripture and tradition, to be formed into persons and a community that God can use for partnership in their vocations and covenant faithfulness in the world."[9]

We have a heritage, ancestors in the faith journey who "have faced critical transitions in the past with stamina, wit, and moral courage to meet 'adaptive challenges'—challenges that require new learning—constructively."[10] In this study we have observed congregations acting prophetically and finding healing and hope. We have described pastors, leaders, and congregations who are able to wade into complexity, and work in concrete and particular ways for a viable future on behalf of us all. In the process of doing extraordinary things for our time they have participated in a kind of learning that has been transformative to their congregations, their communities and themselves.

A theme found in the narratives is the importance of people coming together around the Lord's Table. Our educational model includes transmission of Christian tradition or "schooling," but is equally concerned with a network of multilayered dynamics that join liturgy, proclamation, sharing of joys and concerns, the practice of spiritual disciplines, community discernment. Above all, an intimate spiritual connection in Christ is solidified around the Table as these congregations engaged the hard faith questions at hand.

The "broken-yet-made-whole" symbolism of the Community of Hope is a powerful signifier of the connection between the ability to talk about and address pain and suffering and the ability of a congregation to engage potentially divisive issues as a group. The holding center—or lack thereof—in these congregations was dependent on leadership that can provide a safe environment for disagreement and honesty. But the characteristics of such leaders—the ability to create a holding center, patience, tolerance, ability to frame and reframe issues—always point beyond themselves to communion with Christ and each other as the gathering center of the congregation.

The broken-yet-made-whole chalice beckons from the Table—always there to sustain and to challenge. Following Jesus, we are called to dialogue and discernment—leaving room for the prophetic voices that are hard to hear—as we seek to love kindness, do justice, and walk humbly with our God.

Appendixes

APPENDIX 1 :

RESEARCH QUESTIONS

The following list of questions was drafted using an intensive group process. The questions were used to guide research about the five congregations described in chapters 2 through 6, and also in questionnaires used to gather additional information about thirty-one other Reconciling Congregations.

1) Was there a precipitating event/situation/person that led you to engage in the decision to engage in the RCP study? If so, please describe briefly.

2) What group or groups made the decision? How long were people intentionally involved in a study process before the vote?

3) Briefly outline the process you followed and list the primary resources you used.

4) What was one of the best/most affirming things that happened?

5) What was one of the most difficult/painful things that happened?

6) What has happened in the life of the congregation since the vote that might help us better understand if and/or how your congregation has been able to "embrace difference"?
7) In what ways were children and/or youth involved in and/or affected by this process and decision?
8) Is the pastor(s) who participated in the process still serving in your congregation? If not, how long after the vote did they leave and where did they go?
9) What have you learned about how your congregation might engage in learning about and making decisions on other topics in the future?

OUTLINE OF "ON BECOMING A RECONCILING CONGREGATION" (THE "RED BOOK")

Introduction to the Study Booklet
History of the Church Study of Homosexuality
Personal Statements
Local Area Survey of Attitudes About Homosexuality
Biblical Interpretation of Homosexuality
Reconciling Congregation Statements

REPORT OF THE CONSENSUS SEEKING PROJECT GROUP

The Consensus Seeking Group at Claremont determined the following areas of agreement and disagreement among members of the congregation regarding their ministry to and with lesbians and gay men:

1) When positions are open for Sunday school/Youth Leaders, it is not wise to exclude well-qualified gays and lesbians from consideration.
2) It is important to have dialogue.

3) We do not want to see anyone leave the church because of disagreements on the direction the church will take regarding its ministry with gays and lesbians.
4) Change is not easy.
5) We should make it known that CUMC welcomes everyone, and ministers to the needs of all people.
6) We would like to make it known that gay men and lesbians are welcome at CUMC.

Five areas of disagreement where they could come to no agreement:

1) That CUMC declare itself a Reconciling Congregation and be listed in the national Directory of the Reconciling Congregation Program.
2) We should concentrate on the bonds of Christianity that erase divisions.
3) We should accept the statement in the Discipline about homosexuality being incompatible with Christian teaching.
4) The aforementioned statement in the Discipline is incompatible with Christian teaching and should be changed.
5) CUMC should be a prophetic witness to those who would condemn gays and lesbians.

APPENDIX 4 :

STATEMENT OF RECONCILIATION

The following Statement of Reconciliation was adopted as a guideline for ministry by the Claremont United Methodist Church Council of Ministries, December 15, 1992. It was then discussed at the public church forum on January 7, 1993.

Luke 10:27 says, "you shall love the Lord your God with all your heart, and with all your soul, and with all your strength, and with all your mind; and your neighbor as yourself." In this spirit, we acknowledge that each person is a member of God's family, and a recipient of God's love and grace. Therefore, we members of the Claremont United Methodist Church strive to draw all people into this loving relationship with God, and to be a community which embodies love, reconciliation and justice for all people.

We proclaim that all people are created in the image of God and affirm that all people regardless of age, economic status, ethnicity, gender, abilities, marital status, race, or sexual orientation are beloved children of God.

We seek to insure a world where families are nurtured, children are protected, caring relationships are valued, all people are welcomed, and where silenced voices are heard.

We affirm the inclusion of lesbians and gay men, their families and friends within our church community.

We invite the participation of all people in the life of the church and strive to utilize the many and varied gifts and talents of all members and friends of CUMC.

We acknowledge sexuality as one of God's good gifts to humankind and confess our discomfort with issues related to sexuality.

We pray that the Holy Spirit which calls us to become a reconciling people will continue to create in us at CUMC a vital, active and caring ministry, allowing us with our diverse congregation of young families and children, youth and young adults, middle-aged and older, couples and singles to serve as a model for others.

We profess to be followers of Christ who are seeking to reflect Christ's love through the welcome we extend to all. In the spirit of Christ, we proclaim God's grace and join in a ministry of reconciliation.

BOOKLET OUTLINE

Outline of "Shall We Become a Reconciling Congregation? A Booklet to Help Study the Question," North United Methodist Church, June 1993 (16 pages):

Introduction [written by the Senior Pastor]
Purpose of This Booklet
A Brief History of Homosexuality Issues at North Church
Motion to the North Church Administrative Board
Role and Mission Statement of North Church
What Language Shall We Use? [a glossary of terms including sex, sexuality, homosexuality, homophobia, gay, reconciliation or reconciling, and sexual orientation]
What Is a Reconciling Congregation?
Reconciling Congregation Program Mission Statement
What does *The Book of Discipline* say about homosexuals?

General Conference Action on the Study of Homosexuality and the Church [Things the Church Can Responsibly Teach, Things the Church Cannot Responsibly Teach]

Biblical Interpretation [Literal Views, Traditional Views, Historical and Contextual Views, New Creation Views]

Theological Positions [Homosexuality as a Sin, Homosexuality as Perversion, Homosexuality as Love]

Views of the Human Sciences

References [Books, Videos, Articles, Other Resources]

A Need to Dialogue: How Shall We Tell the Old, Old Story of Jesus and His Love? [a list of titles and times for eight dialogue sessions planned for September 1993 to April 1994]

APPENDIX 6:

THE RITUAL OF "JOINING TOGETHER"

"The Ritual of 'Joining-Together'" from "Toward a Theology of 'Joined-Together,'" the third part of a six page Community of Hope document (no date) that is preceded by "Toward a Theology of 'Joined-Together'" and "Toward an Ethic of 'Joined-Together': Living in Right Relationship."

The rituals of joining-together celebrated in and by our community should reflect not only the wishes of the couple, but also the life and theology of the Community of Hope. There should be no distinction between rituals of joining together for homosexual and heterosexual couples. Therefore, we strongly suggest that any legal action associated with the joining-together, such as signing of marriage licenses and/or powers of attorney, be done at another time and place, and not in connection with the worship ritual.

Since the couple are the ministers of the ritual and God is the one who joins-together, the ritual of joining-together should acknowledge and reflect the role of the community as witnesses. Toward that end, we suggest that the rite include the following elements:

Community Declaration wherein the community declares its intention to witness and to honor the joining-together of the couple.

Examples:

*All:*_____and_____, we rejoice to be part of this celebration, and we are honored to stand as witnesses as you share your vows of commitment to one another.

*All:*_____ and_____, as your family and community, we are honored to be part of this celebration. We have known and loved you individually; we have experienced your being called together by God, and we are honored to stand as witnesses as you share your covenant vows. We affirm your love for one another as holy, and honor your covenant as sacred.

*All:*_____and_____, in our journey together seeking hope, justice and wholeness, those of us who have walked with you as your community of faith have come to know your relationship to be from God. We are grateful to be present to witness and affirm your commitment to one another, and we commit ourselves to honor your relationship and stand in solidarity with you in the struggle for justice, even when the struggle becomes uncomfortable.

One: The joining together of _____and _____ unites their families—given and chosen—and creates a new one. They ask for your blessing.

All: We rejoice in your union, we witness your vows with joy, and we pray God's blessing upon you.

One: Will all of you, by God's grace, do everything in your power to honor, uphold, and care for _____ and _____ in their marriage/union?

All: We will.

Call to Commitment wherein the community invites the couple to share their vows.

Examples:
All: _____ and _____, we rejoice with you on this day and pray for God's blessing on your life together. We now invite you to share your vows of commitment with one another before God and this gathered community!

Community Affirmation wherein the community affirms and celebrates the joining together they have witnessed.

Examples:
One: Vows have been spoken!

All: And rings have been exchanged!

One: A relationship has been blessed, a holy union affirmed!

All: What God has joined together, let no one tear apart.

All: _____ and _____, we have witnessed the sharing of your vows and the giving and receiving of your rings. We affirm your union of love! What God has joined together, let no one tear apart.

All: _____ and _____, we have witnessed and we affirm the joining together of your lives! We commit ourselves to honor your relationship and stand in solidarity with you in the struggle for justice.

Community Blessing wherein the community expresses their hopes for the couple, and their commitment to support the relationship.

Examples:

All: _____and _____, may God bless you with companionship and love from this day forward, and may all who share life with you be blessed by your love.

Laying on of Hands by the whole gathered community.

Words of Blessing offered by one or more members of the community.

Song of Blessing offered by one or more members of the community.

NOTES

1. Introduction: A Guide to Congregational Change

1. The Reconciling Congregation Program was organized in 1984 to guide, provide resources, and support United Methodist congregations considering the possibility of making a public declaration of their intention to welcome all people, including men and women who might otherwise feel excluded because of sexual orientation. In 1999, a Judicial Commission ruled that "a local church or any of its organizational units may not identify or label itself as an unofficial body or movement. Such identification or labeling is subject to the possibility of being in conflict with the [Book of] Discipline and doctrines of The United Methodist Church." This means that no congregation or Annual Conference (a regional body charged with the ordination and appointment of pastors and oversight of congregations in a geographical region) can use the name of an informal movement—such as the Reconciling Congregation Program—in its name. In 2001 the Reconciling Congregation Program expanded its mission and was renamed the Reconciling Ministries Network to reflect a more general set of objectives.

2. The General Conference of The United Methodist Church meets every four years to formulate denominational policy. In the spring of 1996 the General Conference approved the following statement to be added to the *Book of Discipline*: "Ceremonies that celebrate homosexual unions shall not be conducted by our ministers or in our churches." In

the spring of 2000 the General Conference declined a motion to remove the policy from *The Book of Order*.

2. Responding to Tragedy and Injustice

1. Attributed quotes are from my transcriptions of taped interviews with members of the Reconciling Congregation Task Force, church staff, and a member who left the congregation after the decision was made to become a Reconciling Congregation. The interviews were conducted in November, 1995 and April 1997. Unattributed quotes are transcribed from a taped interview in November 1995 with an adult Sunday school class and a luncheon gathering of people who had participated in several phases of exploration of the Reconciling Congregation Program.

2. United Methodism determines church polity in conferences that function as deliberative bodies. The annual conference is the location of ordination and the regional jurisdiction with which United Methodist clergy identify and where they remain members for life. Troy Annual Conference includes congregations in Northeast New York state and all of Vermont.

3. In 1997, the first annual report after becoming a Reconciling Congregation, Saratoga Springs United Methodist Church added 86 members and lost 44 members.

4. This quotation is from an interview with the adult Sunday school class. There were ten men and four women present. Of those, six had been members for twenty-five years or more, five for ten to twenty years, and one "since the class started." There is remarkable continuity among the long-term members who have all served the congregation and Troy Annual Conference in a variety of leadership positions over the years.

5. The Task Force of up to 20 members consisted of people who volunteered their services. Membership varied over the three years of their work together but there were always more women than men. Earlier, several Task Force members had attended training events sponsored by the Conference where they were encouraged to consider Reconciling Congregation Program membership in their congregation. Troy Annual Conference became a Reconciling Conference in 1987 because members disagreed with exclusionary language about homosexuality approved by the 1984 General Conference, the denomination's national policy-making body. Jane Borden led several of the Conference training events.

6. Members of the Task Force and Natalie Bollerud, the Christian education director who recruited and trained Sunday school teachers,

talked about three families who left. Nancy Burdick, a member of one of the families that left after the vote was also a substitute Sunday school teacher, said that eight families left the congregation.

7. Reconciling Congregation Program, Resource Paper #5.

8. Reconciling Congregation Program, Resource Paper #3, p. 3. A new openness in capacity to talk about difficult issues like human sexuality is considered a major enrichment of community life that should follow from extended discussions in a congregation exploring the possibility of becoming a Reconciling Congregation.

9. Ibid.

3. Following a Tradition: Seeking a Vision

1. There is some fluidity in the organizational structure of United Methodist congregations. Some have both an Administrative Council or Board and a Council of Ministries, while others have only an Administrative Council. There is also fluidity in how a particular congregation makes a decision such as whether or not to join the RCP. Each congregation in this study used a slightly different decision-making procedure.

2. Larry B. Stammer, "Debating Faith and Sexuality," *Los Angeles Times*, 22 February 2000, p. 1.

4. Making the Implicit Explicit: The Fence Around Hospitality

1. Jim Herrington, Mike Bonem, and James H. Furr, *Leading Congregational Change: A Practical Guide for the Transformational Journey* (San Francisco: Jossey-Bass, 2000), pp. 96-97.

2. Harvey and Lois Seifert, *When Christians Disagree* (Prescott, Ariz.: Education Ministries, Inc., 1991).

3. The author spent considerable time looking through Minute Books of North's Administrative Board doing research for this chapter. Records of the establishment of an "executive committee" for the board or "minutes" of such a group were not found. The writer remembered a discussion at an earlier board meeting in which the senior pastor suggested the wisdom of such a committee for his guidance when issues might arise for his decision making, for example, groups who some might consider controversial seeking use of the building. One of the

most senior men replied that the pastor seemed to be calling them well by himself. No action was taken.

4. The sermon selections were transcribed from a tape recording of the worship service for June 8, 1997.

5. From an address to leaders, "Leading from Within: Reflections on Spirituality and Leadership."

6. Creating a New Tradition: The Broken Made Whole

1. Because the Community of Hope was not formally a member of the Annual Conference, and because of their intention to be nonhierarchical, they chose to refer to themselves as "companions" rather than "members" of the community.

2. Each Annual Conference is organized, governed, and supervised by a bishop and several district superintendents who are each responsible for a district within the Conference. The cabinet of the Conference includes the bishop, the superintendents, and support staff.

8. Claiming Ministries of Compassion and Justice: Being the Body of Christ

1. Paul D. Hanson, *The People Called: The Growth of Community in the Bible* (San Francisco: Harper & Row, 1986), p. 236.

2. Ibid., p. 275.

3. Ibid., p. 535.

4. Ibid., pp. 69-70.

5. Eric H. F. Law, *Inclusion: Making Room for Grace* (St. Louis: Chalice Press, 2000), pp. 42-43.

6. Ellen J. Langer, *The Power of Mindful Learning* (Reading, Mass.: Addison-Wesley, 1997), p. 4.

7. Laurent A. Parks Daloz, "Transformative Learning for the Common Good," in Jack Mezirow, *Learning as Transformation: Critical Perspectives on a Theory in Progress* (San Francisco: Jossey-Bass, 2000), p. 5.

8. Mary Field Belenky et al., *Women's Ways of Knowing* (New York: Basic Books, 1986), pp. 143-46.

9. Jack Mezirow, "Learning to Think Like An Adult: Core Concepts of Transformation Theory," in Jack Mezirow, *Learning as Transformation:*

Critical Perspectives on a Theory in Progress (San Francisco: Jossey-Bass, 2000), pp. 12-13.

10. Ibid., pp. 18-19.

11. Hanson, *The People Called,* p. 535.

9. Congregations Reformed and Renewed: The Broken-Yet-Made-Whole Body of Christ

1. George Lakoff and Mark Johnson, *Metaphors We Live By* (Chicago: University of Chicago Press, 1980), p. 193.

2. We agree with conclusions stated in Nancy Tatom Ammerman, ed., *Congregation and Community* (New Brunswick, N.J.: Rutgers University Press, 1997), pp. 343-45. She writes that in congregations where change has occurred what matters is not which ideas congregations draw on, but whether they are able to engage in the work of reshaping these ideas for a new situation.

3. Renate Caine and Geoffrey Caine, *Making Connections: Teaching and the Human Brain* (Nashville: Abingdon Press, 1991), pp. 63-78.

4. Donald P. McNeill et al., *Compassion: A Reflection on the Christian Life* (Garden City, N.Y.: Doubleday, 1982).

5. Eric H. F. Law, *Inclusion: Making Room for Grace* (St. Louis: Chalice Press, 2000), pp. 39-47.

6. Loren Mead, *Transforming Congregations for the Future* (Bethesda, Md.: Alban Institute, 1994), p. 17.

7. Thomas Hawkins, *The Learning Congregation* (Louisville: Westminster John Knox Press, 1997), p. 141.

8. Elizabeth Box Price, "Cognitive Complexity and the Learning Congregation" (paper presented for the Association of Professors and Researchers in Religious Education, Toronto, Canada, 1999).

9. James Fowler, *Weaving the New Creation* (San Francisco: HarperSanFrancisco, 1991), pp. 189-90. See also James Fowler, *Faithful Change* (Nashville: Abingdon Press, 1996).

10. Laurent A. Parks Daloz et al., *Common Fire: Leading Lives of Commitment in a Complex World* (Boston: Beacon Press, 1996), p. 5.

BIBLIOGRAPHY

Ammerman, Nancy Tatom et al. *Congregation and Community*. New Brunswick: Rutgers University Press, 1997.

————. Jackson W. Carroll, Carl S. Dudley, William McKinney, eds. *Studying Congregations: A New Handbook*. Nashville: Abingdon Press, 1998.

Belenky, Mary Field et al. *Women's Ways of Knowing*. New York: Basic Books, 1986.

Caine, Renate and Geoffrey Caine. *Making Connections: Teaching and the Human Brain*. Nashville: Abingdon Press, 1990.

Daloz, Laurent A. Parks et al. *Common Fire: Leading Lives of Commitment in a Complex World*. Boston: Beacon Press, 1997.

Daloz, Laurent A. Parks. "Transformative Learning for the Common Good," in Mezirow, Jack. *Learning as Transformation: Critical Perspectives on a Theory in Progress*. San Francisco: Jossey-Bass, 2000, pp. 103-24.

Foster, Charles R. *Educating Congregations*. Nashville: Abingdon Press, 1994.

Fowler, James W. *Faithful Change*. Nashville: Abingdon Press, 1996.

————. *Weaving the New Creation*. San Francisco: HarperSanFrancisco, 1991.

Gaede, Beth Ann, ed. *Congregations Talking About Homosexuality*. Bethesda, Md.: Alban Institute, 1998.

Hanson, Paul D. *The People Called: The Growth of Community in the Bible*. San Francisco: Harper & Row, 1986.

Hartman, Keith. *Congregations in Conflict: The Battle over Homosexuality*. New Brunswick: Rutgers University Press, 1996.

Hawkins, Thomas R. *The Learning Congregation*. Louisville: Westminster John Knox, 1997.

Herrington, Jim, Mike Bonem, and James H. Furr. *Leading Congregational*

Change: A Practical Guide for the Transformational Journey. San Francisco: Jossey-Bass, 2000.

Kegan, Robert. "What 'Form' Transforms: A Constructive-Developmental Approach to Transformative Living," in Mezirow, Jack, *Learning as Transformation*. San Francisco: Jossey-Bass, 2000, pp. 35-69.

Lakoff, George and Mark Johnson. *Metaphors We Live By*. Chicago: University of Chicago Press, 1980.

Langer, Ellen J. *The Power of Mindful Learning*. Reading, Mass.: Addison-Wesley, 1997.

Law, Eric H. F. *Inclusion: Making Room for Grace*. St. Louis: Chalice Press, 2000.

McNeill, Donald P. et al. *Compassion, a Reflection on the Christian Life*. Garden City, N.Y.: Doubleday, 1982.

Mead, Loren B. *Transforming Congregations for the Future*. Bethesda, Md.: Alban Institute, 1994.

Mezirow, Jack. *Learning as Transformation: Critical Perspectives on a Theory in Progress*. San Francisco: Jossey-Bass, 2000.

————. "Learning to Think Like an Adult: Core Concepts of Transformation Theory," in Mezirow, Jack. *Learning as Transformation*. San Francisco: Jossey-Bass, 2000, pp. 3-33.

Palmer, Parker J. *To Know as We Are Known: A Spirituality of Education*. San Francisco: Harper & Row, 1983.

Sample, Tex and Amy E. DeLong, eds. *The Loyal Opposition: Struggling with the Church on Homosexuality*. Nashville: Abingdon Press, 2000.

Seifert, Harvey and Lois Seifert. *When Christians Disagree*. Prescott, Ariz.: Education Ministries, 1991.

Wind, James P. and James W. Lewis, eds. *American Congregations*. Chicago: University of Chicago Press, 1994.

Wood, James R. *Where the Spirit Leads: The Evolving Views of United Methodists on Homosexuality*. Nashville: Abingdon Press, 2000.